A More Profound Alleluia

The CALVIN INSTITUTE OF CHRISTIAN WORSHIP LITURGICAL STUDIES Series, edited by John D. Witvliet, is designed to promote reflection on the history, theology, and practice of Christian worship and to stimulate worship renewal in Christian congregations. Contributions include writings by pastoral worship leaders from a wide range of communities and scholars from a wide range of disciplines. The ultimate goal of these contributions is to nurture worship practices that are spiritually vital and theologically rooted.

Published

Gather into One: Praying and Singing Globally
C. Michael Hawn

The Substance of Things Seen: Art, Faith, and the Christian Community
Robin M. Jensen

Wonderful Words of Life: Hymns in American Protestant History and Theology
Richard J. Mouw and Mark A Noll, Editors

Discerning the Spirits:
A Guide to Thinking about Christian Worship Today
Cornelius Plantinga Jr. and Sue A. Rozeboom

Voicing God's Psalms
Calvin Seerveld

My Only Comfort: Death, Deliverance, and Discipleship
in the Music of Bach
Calvin R. Stapert

A More Profound Alleluia: Theology and Worship in Harmony
Leanne Van Dyk, Editor

Christian Worship in Reformed Churches Past and Present
Lukas Vischer, Editor

A More Profound Alleluia

Theology and Worship in Harmony

Edited by

Leanne Van Dyk

WILLIAM B. EERDMANS PUBLISHING COMPANY

GRAND RAPIDS, MICHIGAN / CAMBRIDGE, U.K.

© 2005 Wm. B. Eerdmans Publishing Co.

Wm. B. Eerdmans Publishing Co.
255 Jefferson Ave. S.E., Grand Rapids, Michigan 49503 /
P.O. Box 163, Cambridge CB3 9PU U.K.

Printed in the United States of America

10 09 08 07 06 05   9 8 7 6 5 4 3

ISBN-10: 0-8028-2854-X
ISBN-13: 978-0-8028-2854-5

www.eerdmans.com

Contents

Ending of Worship ≈ Ethics   133
David L. Stubbs

Series Preface

Making Connections

Christian corporate worship is an integrating practice at the center of the Christian life. It both reflects and shapes our view of God, the world, and their relations. It grounds, sharpens, and humbles the work the church does in every sphere of ministry, including education, pastoral care, evangelism, and justice. And it gathers up every facet of our lives before God's face — at work and play; at home, school, and marketplace; in times of joy and sorrow — and then sends us out to live in obedience and joy.

Part of our mandate at the Calvin Institute of Christian Worship, and in this series of books, is to make the connections between worship and the various facets of Christian thought and life explicit and instructive in ways that promote deeper and more vital worship practices. This particular volume highlights arguably the most important connections that need to be made for worship to be well grounded — namely, the connections between our liturgical actions and our understanding of the God we worship. After all, as D. A. Carson has observed, "worship" is a transitive verb.[1] What is important is not *that* we worship, but rather that we worship *God*. For all our talk about "grounding worship in theol-

1. D. A. Carson, "'Worship the Lord Your God': The Perennial Challenge," in *Worship: Adoration and Action* (Grand Rapids: Baker Academic, 1993), p. 15.

ogy," most Christians (and even Christian leaders) actually spend very little energy working at it. By and large, most of us accept ideas about God, salvation, and the church that are in the cultural air we breathe, and we worship in ways that make us most comfortable. This book, however, aims at "a more profound alleluia," a vision that is at once biblical, compelling, and spiritually nourishing.

Hymns

A particular virtue of this study is the frequent use of recently written hymn texts to explore a particular theme or idea. Though much maligned in recent years, traditional patterns of hymnody offer a rich resource for both worship and theology. They convey central and distinctive Christian insights in ways that are both accessible and memorable.

It would likely be a surprise to many worshipers that more hymns have been written in traditional forms in the past generation than in any other period in Protestant history, with the possible exception of the last several years of Charles Wesley's life. Indeed, our time has witnessed what some observers have called "The Hymn Renaissance" — an ecumenical resurgence of hymnwriting that has resulted in a bevy of new hymnals, hymnal supplements, single-author hymn collections, and hymnwriting workshops. One very good place to sense this activity is in the work of the The Hymn Society in the United States and Canada and in its periodical *The Hymn,* which includes references to the publication of over seventy single-author hymn collections in the past two decades. The hymns included in this volume represent many of the leading hymnwriters of our time.[2]

The hymns printed here, following each chapter, are primarily intended for reflection and meditation. Indeed, hymn poems are a wonder-

2. For more on this "Hymn Renaissance," see William Lock, "Congregational Singing in England, Canada, and the United States since 1950," in *The Complete Library of Christian Worship,* ed. Robert E. Webber (Nashville: Star Song Publishing Group, 1994), vol. 4, book 1, p. 270; and Paul Westermeyer, "Singing New Hymns," in *Sing! A New Creation,* Leaders' Edition (Grand Rapids: CRC Publications, 2002), p. 412.

ful resource for devotional use by individuals, families, groups, and congregations. Worship leaders should consider recommending one hymn text per week for private or group reflection and then singing the hymn in worship as a simple way of connecting private and corporate worship.

Hymn texts are also invaluable in the study of both Christian history and theology. They reveal in highly focused and memorable ways the particular insights, passions, metaphors, and tendencies of their authors. My own students know that each of my examinations will include at least one hymn poem for them to analyze — a practice that fosters the wonderful habit of giving thoughtful consideration to the words we sing and of perceiving more clearly the connections between worship and worldview.

But most importantly, hymns are meant to be sung, and sung in worshiping communities. Each of the hymns included in this book sings well. Though these texts are included in more than one recently published hymnal, having access to four particular hymnals — the *Psalter Hymnal,* the *Presbyterian Hymnal,* the *Lutheran Book of Worship,* and *Sing! A New Creation* — will give you access to settings with printed music.[3]

The presence of these hymns also suggests that this book can be used in ways that bring study and worship together. Study groups and worship committees who discuss each essay over time can conclude

---

3. *Psalter Hymnal* (Grand Rapids: CRC Publications, 1987); *Presbyterian Hymnal* (Louisville: Westminster/John Knox Press, 1990); *Lutheran Book of Worship* (Minneapolis: Augsburg Publishing House, 1978); *Sing! A New Creation* (Grand Rapids: Faith Alive Publications, 2002). To order these (or any other in-print hymnal), simply contact the Hymn Society at 1-800-THE-HYMN or www.thehymnsociety.org.

Otherwise, compare the meter indications, which give you the number of syllables per hymn line, with the metrical index of any major hymnal for possible tunes for each text. Meters for the hymns included after each chapter are as follows: "Come, Great God of All the Ages," 8.7.8.7 D; "God the Spirit, Guide and Guardian," 8.7.8.7 D; "We Cannot Measure How You Heal," LMD; "Children from Your Vast Creation," 8.7.8.7 D; "Thanks to God Whose Word Was Spoken," 8.7.8.7.4.4.7; "Thy Strong Word," 8.7.8.7 D; "O Christ, the Great Foundation," 7.6.7.6 D; "Our Cities Cry to You, O God," CMD; "Remembering with Love and Hope," CM; "I Come with Joy, a Child of God," CM; "Lord, Whose Love in Humble Service," 8.7.8.7 D; and "Canto de Esperanza/Song of Hope," 1.11.11.11 with refrain. Choosing a fitting hymn tune is a delicate task that involves more than meter; the spirit and shape of the tune must also fit the text.

their study in song. Pastors who don't use the revised common
lectionary to guide their choice of preaching texts might consider a series of sermons on the six themes of this book. The hymns included here
will make preparing for worship those weeks a bit easier. Students who
are assigned to read these essays might find that the hymn texts published here will serve to blur the distinction between theological study
and prayer that sometimes characterizes the study of theology, re-
integrating what need not be divided.

Acknowledgments

We are particularly grateful for the wise and careful leadership of
Leanne Van Dyk at every stage of this project. We are grateful for all the
contributors, and for their eager participation in two memorable colloquium meetings. And we thank Robert Nordling and Cherith Fee
Nordling for significant contributions in colloquium discussions.

This work is possible because of the generosity of the Lilly Endow-
ment and because of its Vice President for Religion, Craig Dykstra. His
vision for practical theology that forms and deepens the Christian life is
a welcome invitation and challenge to all of us who research and teach in
any subdiscipline of theological studies.

I am particularly grateful for the faithful work of Worship Institute
staff members who enable our collaborative research projects. Kristen
Verhulst, Joyce Borger, Cindy Holtrop, and Emily Cooper were especially
helpful at various stages of this project.

Finally, we thank Eerdmans Publishing Company and its Senior Vice
President, Jon Pott, for collaboration on this and other volumes in our
series. Their editorial work is a ministry of Christian education and formation that enriches the work of many readers worldwide.

JOHN D. WITVLIET
Calvin Institute of Christian Worship
Calvin College and Calvin Theological Seminary
Grand Rapids, Michigan

Contributors

Ronald P. Byars is Professor of Preaching and Worship at Union Theological Seminary–Presbyterian School of Christian Education in Richmond, Virginia. He is the author of *The Future of Protestant Worship: Beyond the Worship Wars* (Westminster/John Knox Press, 2002), and is currently working on a book on Eucharistic prayer in the Reformed tradition.

William A. Dyrness is Professor of Theology and Culture at Fuller Theological Seminary and a founding member of its Brehm Center for Worship, Theology, and the Arts. He is the author of *Visual Faith: Art, Theology, and Worship in Dialogue* (Baker Academic, 2001) and, most recently, *Reformed Theology and Visual Culture: The Protestant Imagination from Calvin to Edwards* (Cambridge University Press, 2004).

Martha L. Moore-Keish is Assistant Professor of Theology at Columbia Theological Seminary in Decatur, Georgia. She was previously an associate in the Office of Theology and Worship of the Presbyterian Church (USA) and Assistant Professor of Liturgical Studies at Yale Divinity School and the Yale Institute of Sacred Music. Her current research interests include the issue of open communion and the conversation between feminist and baptismal theologies.

David L. Stubbs is Assistant Professor of Ethics and Theology at Western Theological Seminary in Holland, Michigan. He is currently writing a book on the idea of participation in Christ in Karl Barth's theology.

Leanne Van Dyk is Academic Dean and Professor of Reformed Theology at Western Theological Seminary in Holland, Michigan. Her books are *The Desire of Divine Love: The Theology of John McLeod Campbell* (Peter Lang Publishers, 1995) and *Believing in Jesus Christ*, a volume in the "Foundations" series, sponsored by the Office of Theology and Worship of the Presbyterian Church (USA) (Geneva Press, 2002).

John D. Witvliet is Director of the Calvin Institute of Christian Worship and holds faculty appointments in worship, theology, and music at both Calvin College and Calvin Theological Seminary in Grand Rapids, Michigan. He is the author of *Worship Seeking Understanding* (Baker Academic, 2003) and co-editor of *Worship in Medieval and Early Modern Europe* (University of Notre Dame Press, 2004).

Introduction

Christians are called by God to worship, to do so with one another and in the company of Jesus Christ. It is in worship that our lives are formed by the Holy Spirit and informed by God's Word. It is in worship that our theology is shaped, our discipleship encouraged, and our spirits fed by the good food of word and sacrament. It is from worship that we are sent out into the world to continue to live the patterns of life we have begun to learn and practice in worship. Worship is, for Christians, both "primary school" and "graduate school" — a place where we are always learning the basics of how to be in true relationship to God and yet also reaching for the advanced skills we need for obedient and faithful Christian lives.

Worship is, therefore, a Christian activity of the highest importance. Because of this, worship is worthy of our careful thought and reflection. Theology, too, is a Christian activity that requires the very best from us. Theology is not an enterprise only for specialists; in fact, William Placher says that "all Christians do theology all the time."[1] When a Christian parent wonders why her child contracts a rare illness, cannot find an answer, but confesses that God has been present in gracious ways throughout the ordeal, that is frontline theology. When the worship committee of a congregation disputes sharply over how prominent intercessory prayer should be in worship, or how to distribute the ele-

1. *Essentials of Christian Theology*, ed. William Placher (Louisville: Westminster/John Knox Press, 2003), p. 1.

ments at communion, or whether the communion table should be moved aside for the praise band, they are engaging basic theological issues as well. Some Christian persons and communities are highly self-reflective of their theological underpinnings. Others are less reflective, less aware of the theological currents that run deep beneath their practices and assumptions. One of the goals of this book is to make clear the connections between theology and worship — to make explicit the many implicit theological assumptions of worship practices and to draw out the rich worship practices implicit in the treasures of the Christian theological traditions.

> **The first and basic act of theological work is <u>prayer</u>.**
>
> Karl Barth

A further goal of this book is to join the conversation with those interested in and committed to theology and worship, a conversation that has been growing more lively and interesting in recent years. Several generations ago, this conversation was only imagined by an interdisciplinary few. Theology was a discipline unto itself. Worship was the realm of practitioners. But this is an artificial divide. The best theology has always been deeply doxological and the best worship richly theological. Consider the tradition of superb hymns. Hymn texts are super-concentrated theology, treasures of compact theological statement. The church that sings excellent hymn texts — even more, the people that are fortunate enough to memorize excellent hymn texts — are being formed in a fine school of faith.

The deep integrations of theology and worship that have always found voice in the text and music of a first-rate hymn are being examined once again by liturgical theologians, systematic theologians, and pastors who want to engage their congregations in theologically coherent patterns of worship. What is being discovered anew are the many natural and nuanced ways that one's theology impacts one's worship and one's worship impacts one's theology.[2]

2. See, for example, Geoffrey Wainwright, *Doxology: A Systematic Theology* (New York: Oxford University Press, 1980); Don E. Saliers, *Worship as Theology: Foretaste of Glory Divine*

The authors decided to organize the book by juxtaposing a moment in the liturgy with a corresponding theological doctrine. We attempted to explore how a particular moment in the liturgy and a particular theological doctrine could fruitfully illuminate each other. Six liturgical moments were chosen and paired with six doctrines. The opening of worship was paired with the doctrine of the Trinity. Confession and assurance were paired with the doctrines of sin and grace. Creeds and prayers were paired with ecclesiology. The proclamation of the Word of God, including Scripture and sermon, was paired with revelation and Christology. Eucharist was paired with eschatology. The ending of worship, the benediction and charge, was paired with ethics.

> It is imperative to recognize the essence of theology as lying in the liturgical action of adoration, thanksgiving, and petition.
>
> Karl Barth

The structure of this book is, in many ways, an experiment in juxtaposition. We are convinced that theology and worship are rightly and fruitfully related. Yet we are well aware that the lines of connection are far more numerous than the ones that have been drawn in the table of contents here! These juxtapositions are illustrative, not exhaustive. We know, for example, that the doctrine of the Trinity informs far more than just the opening of worship. We are attentive to the fact that ethics is the beating heart of the entire liturgy, not just the benediction and charge. We are alert to the Christological implications of the assurance of pardon and the sacraments, not only the sermon and the reading of Scripture. The structure of the book — liturgical moment paired with

---

(Nashville: Abingdon, 1994); Gordon Lathrop's trilogy: *Holy Things: A Liturgical Theology; Holy People: A Liturgical Ecclesiology;* and *Holy Ground: A Liturgical Cosmology* (Minneapolis: Fortress Press, 1993, 1999, and 2003, respectively); *To Glorify God: Essays on Modern Reformed Liturgy,* ed. Bryan D. Spinks and Iain R. Torrance (Grand Rapids: Eerdmans, 1999); and *Primary Sources of Liturgical Theology: A Reader,* ed. Dwight Vogel (Collegeville, Minn.: Liturgical Press, 2000).

doctrine — offers only a starting place for a full accounting of the integration of theology and worship.

The theological implications of liturgy and the liturgical implications of theology are a rich and beautiful mosaic. In the organization of this book, we have lifted up one simple scheme to illustrate and amplify our core conviction: at its best, theology has always been done doxologically; at its best, worship has always been done with theological thoughtfulness.

In order to explore the links between theology and worship, then, the authors have asked these kinds of questions in the chapters: How can the doctrine of the Trinity help a pastor or liturgist plan the call to worship and the opening praise hymns? Or, conversely, how can excellent worship music shape and inform the doctrine of the Trinity? What are the contributions of liturgical confessions of sin to our own theological understanding of reality? How does the doctrine of the Incarnation help us understand the reading of Scripture in the worship service? When we celebrate the Lord's Supper on a Sunday morning, what connection are we making with the coming reign of God? When the minister sends us out with the familiar words of the benediction, what ethics does that bind upon us? What particular responsibility toward God, toward each other, and toward the world ripples out from the benediction and charge?

> One can't tap the finger of liturgy without immediately getting the whole hand of theology.
>
> Gerardus van der Leeuw

The theological questions of worship practices and the worship implications of theology have always been present for those alert enough to notice them. Indeed, even casual observers of worship services know how deeply embedded theology is in worship. Consider the opening of the worship service. Does a worship service begin with the announcements by a worship leader? Or does it start with a call to worship drawn from the Psalms — "Our help is in the name of the Lord, who created heaven and earth"? There is a theology at play in both of those openings, an understanding, explicit or implicit, about what fundamentally is happening in worship.

Or consider how the offering is handled in the worship service. Is it collected at the door as worshipers come in to the church? Is it collected during the worship service by the deacons, who then disappear into another room with the collection baskets? Or is it collected during the worship service by the deacons, who then present the offering — perhaps while the congregation sings the *Gloria Patri* or another hymn of thanksgiving — to the minister or elders at the front of the sanctuary? Each of these possible options has a theological corollary.

> We are connected to and drawn into the Christian faith's disclosure of the triune God's hospitality and truth through two modes of reception: worship and doctrine.
>
> Reinhard Hütter

Just as worship expressions have theological implications, theology must find its own fruitful implications for worship. Theological reflection that remains aloof from the embodied and particularized life of faith in the church will fail to serve the church. In the context of a contemporary church, which often is dubious about the importance of theology, the emerging conversation between theology and worship gives the theologian a unique opportunity to demonstrate the genuine vitality of theology engaged for the sake of the church. Alexander Schmemann puts it quite bluntly: "Theology cannot recover its central place and function within the church without being rooted again in the very experience of the Church (in thanksgiving and supplication)."[3]

Don Saliers notes that the dependence of theology on worship runs so deep in the theology of Karl Barth that "critical theological thinking is secondary and therefore derivative of the first-order theology shown in

3. Alexander Schmemann, "Liturgy and Theology," *Greek Orthodox Theological Review* 17, no. 1 (Spring 1972): 100. See also *Practicing Theology*, ed. Miroslav Volf and Dorothy C. Bass (Grand Rapids: Eerdmans, 2002), especially Reinhard Hütter's essay entitled "Hospitality and Truth: The Disclosure of Practices in Worship and Doctrine," pp. 206-27.

praying to God."[4] The image of first-order theology as prayer captures the mutual relationships explored in this book. It is the conviction of the authors that the theological implications of worship and the worship implications of theology are worthy of careful reflection. We imagine congregations who plan worship with thoughtful theological integrity, asking questions about the theological implications of their worship practices. We imagine theologians who ask questions about the worship implications of their theology. We dare to dream that the interdisciplinary conversation will enrich both sides of the equation — that both theologians and worship leaders will learn to sing a more profound "allelulia" to the praise and glory of God, who calls us to worship in spirit and in truth.

LEANNE VAN DYK

4. Saliers, *Worship as Theology*, p. 71.

The Opening of Worship | Trinity

John D. Witvliet

When I was a little boy, I naively thought that God lived behind — or at least beyond — the stained-glass window at the front of my church. This was a beautiful, neo-Gothic church, with lovely stained-glass windows, including a round one located up front near the ceiling. I thought that God lived there because that's where our attention was implicitly directed. We sang our hymns of praise and thanks while facing the front of church, to God "on high." Our offerings were carried forward. Everything we did implicitly reinforced the notion that as we worshiped, God was "before us" or "above us."

I know that the experience of some of my students is quite different. Their journal entries suggest that they tend to imagine that in worship God dwells "in their hearts." In worship, they expectantly wait for a warm emotional experience that confirms it. They know, of course, that God is not contained inside them. Still, they implicitly sense that God is present most fully in worship as the One who lives within them.

C. S. Lewis addressed this question of how Christians conceive of God in a brief commentary on the doctrine of the Trinity. Eager to explain how Trinitarian theology is not merely abstract or mathematical but can be experiential, Lewis wrote,

---

I am grateful to Joyce Borger and Nathan Sytsma for research assistance in preparing this chapter.

1

You may ask, "If we cannot imagine a three-personal Being, what is the good of talking about Him?" Well, there isn't any good talking about Him. The thing that matters is being actually drawn into that three-personal life, and that may begin any time — tonight, if you like. What I mean is this. An ordinary simple Christian kneels down to say his prayers. He is trying to get into touch with God. But if a Christian, he knows that what is prompting him to pray is also God: God, so to speak, inside him. But he also knows that all his real knowledge of God comes through Christ, the Man who was God — that Christ is standing beside him, helping him to pray, praying for him. You see what is happening. God is the thing to which he is praying — the goal he is trying to reach. God is also the thing inside him which is pushing him on — the motive power. God is also the road or bridge along which he is being pushed to that goal. So that the whole three-fold life of the three-personal being is actually going on in that ordinary little bedroom where an ordinary Christian is saying his prayers.[1]

This is a different and altogether remarkable way of imagining God. In this way of thinking, God is not only the One before us, "up there" to receive our praise. God is also "alongside us" in the person of Jesus, perfecting our otherwise imperfect songs and prayers. God is also at work "within us," prodding us, prompting us, encouraging us, and even — when we are unable to pray — praying through us (Rom. 8:26). "It is one experience of God," as Sarah Coakley describes it, "but God as simultaneously (i) doing the praying in me, (ii) receiving that prayer, and (iii) in that exchange, consented to in me, inviting me into the Christic life of redeemed sonship."[2]

This is a vision of God that is, we might say, geographically complex. God inhabits three places in our imagination at the same time (which is, of course, harder for us to imagine than for God to accomplish!). Though it would be wrongly self-centered to say that we are at "the cen-

1. C. S. Lewis, *Mere Christianity* (New York: Touchstone, 1943), p. 143.
2. Sarah Coakley, "Living into the Mystery of the Holy Trinity: Trinity, Prayer, and Sexuality," *Anglican Theological Review* 80 (1998): 224.

ter" of this activity, it may be helpful to picture ourselves right there "in the middle" of it. Or to ponder Robert Jenson's evocative image: "The particular God of Scripture does not just stand over against us; he envelops us."[3] In this vision, we still pray and sing "to" each divine person "Holy, holy, holy . . . blessed Trinity!", but we are also aware that we pray and sing "through Christ," "in the power of the Spirit."[4]

This is also a remarkably active vision of God. The picture here is not of God as a passive being up in heaven, waiting for us to sing a little louder and pray a little harder before conferring a blessing. That description better fits Baal! (1 Kings 18). No, God is active in prompting our worship, in receiving it, and in perfecting it.

The Trinitarian Grammar or Logic of Worship

The doctrine of the Trinity serves as a "grammar" to organize how we describe both divine life and the relationship with God we are privileged to share. This "Trinitarian grammar" draws together and depends on several scriptural themes.

First, there are the biblical texts that explain the theological dynamics of our speech to God — that is, all of our prayers, praise, and thanksgiving. God is the One who receives our worship, as Jesus' familiar words in John 4:24 simply assume: "Those who worship the Father . . . worship in spirit and in truth." Jesus Christ, the second person of the Trinity, is the One who perfects our worship. Just as Hebrew priests represented the people of Israel before God, so Jesus represents us before God "because Jesus lives forever, he has a permanent priesthood.

3. Robert Jenson, *Triune Identity: God According to the Gospel* (Philadelphia: Fortress Press, 1982), p. 51.

4. The two primary models for Christian prayer and worship are (1) prayer directed to God the Father, God the Son, and God the Holy Spirit, and (2) prayer directed to the Father, through Christ, in the Spirit. For more on these models, see Josef Jungmann, *The Place of Christ in Liturgical Prayer*, trans. A. Peeler (Staten Island, N.Y.: Alba House, 1965), and Graham Redding, *Prayer and the Priesthood of Christ in the Reformed Tradition* (London: T&T Clark, 2003).

Therefore he is able to save completely those who come to God through him, because he always lives to intercede for them" (Heb. 7:23-25). The Holy Spirit is the One who prompts our prayer in the first place: "[by him] we cry 'Abba, Father'"; and when we are too weak to pray, "the Spirit himself intercedes for us with groans that words cannot express" (Rom. 8:15, 26).

> The God whom we adore on Trinity Sunday is the Three-Personed God whose own inner core of being is love and whose nature it is to give that love to his creatures without restraint, without measure, without calculation, without ceasing.
>
> Fleming Rutledge

These themes come together in the straightforward Pauline assertion that "through Christ we both [Jew and Gentile] have access to the Father by one Spirit" (Eph. 2:18). We might call this pattern the Trinitarian grammar or logic of our address to God, the "human-Godward" aspect of worship.

Second, there are the biblical texts that reveal the theological dynamics of God's speech to us. A Trinitarian pattern can be perceived here as well. God is the One who sends the Spirit to prompt us. "God has sent the Spirit of his Son into our hearts, crying, 'Abba! Father!'" (Gal. 4:6). Jesus Christ is the "content" of God's speaking to us. He is the "Word" who comes to us "full of grace and truth" (John 1:1, 14), "the radiance of God's glory and the exact representation of his being" (Heb. 1:3). God the Holy Spirit is the One who prompts us to hear God speaking to us. "We have received . . . the Spirit who is from God, that we may understand what God has freely given us" (1 Cor. 2:12). Thus, the "God-humanward" speech also has a Trinitarian shape.

So both human-divine and divine-human communication work out of Trinitarian logic. No wonder so many Christian theologians have developed tight, symmetrical Trinitarian definitions of worship. Thomas F. Torrance, for example, describes worship this way: "In our worship the Holy Spirit comes forth from God, uniting us to the response and obedience and faith and prayer of Jesus, and returns to God, raising us up in

Jesus to participate in the worship of heaven and in the eternal communion of the Holy Trinity."[5]

The Doctrine of the Trinity as Fundamental and Distinctive

This Trinitarian way of thinking has very deep roots in the Christian tradition. For many Christians who stand in the long tradition of classical
or orthodox Christianity, the doctrine of the Trinity is a fundamental
way of thinking about God.[6] It is at once one of the most complex, luminous, and perhaps misunderstood of all Christian doctrines. Yet Trinity
doctrine is based on scriptural assertions about divine identity that
ground the kind of Trinitarian grammar already described:

1. The Bible teaches that there is One God, the God of Abraham and
   Sarah and their offspring, the One who created the world and redeemed the people of Israel: "The Lord our God is one" (Deut. 6:4).
   This means that we don't have to worry that there are divided loyalties or competing interests in divine life.
2. The Bible teaches that Jesus Christ is a divine person, the One who
   was with God in the beginning, and, in fact, was God (John 1:1). This
   Jesus Christ is the "exact representation of God's being" (Heb. 1:1),
   and the perfect image or "icon" of God (Col. 1:15).
3. The Bible strongly suggests, and traditional Christian theology in-
   sists, that the Holy Spirit is also a divine person (Acts 5:3-4; 2 Cor.
   13:14).[7]

5. Thomas Torrance, *Theology in Reconstruction* (Grand Rapids: Eerdmans, 1965),
p. 250.

6. In the words of James Buckley and David Yeago, "In accounting for Christian trin-
itarianism, one is up against the deep structures of Christian identity, with that which is
constitutive of what is 'Christian' in a profound and epistemically basic way." See *Knowing
the Triune God: The Work of the Spirit in the Practices of the Church* (Grand Rapids: Eerdmans,
2001), p. 15.

7. Cornelius Plantinga Jr., "Trinity," in *The International Standard Bible Encyclopedia*, ed.
Geoffrey W. Bromiley, vol. 4 (Grand Rapids: Eerdmans, 1988), pp. 914-21.

When the early church put these biblical assertions together, the result was the doctrine of the Trinity, a doctrine that slowly emerged through centuries of theological reflection, often colored by competing philosophical and political interests. Key steps in this reflection were the church councils that produced carefully formulated creedal summaries of the Christian faith, including the Nicene Creed in A.D. 381, and the Athanasian Creed, which developed in the Latin West after the time of Augustine. The theme that echoes through these documents, and early theologians like Athanasius and Augustine, can be summed up in this concise way: "The Father is God, the Son is God, the Holy Spirit is God; yet, there are not three gods, but one God."[8]

Interestingly, conversations about worship and prayer were among the most important parts of these early church discussions of the Trinity. One of the pastoral questions that prompted the church's reflection on the identity of Jesus and the Holy Spirit was directly related to prayer and worship.[9] Was it legitimate to worship Christ as fully divine — and to pray to Christ? If so, then what about the Holy Spirit? The early church answered "yes" to both questions. As a result, many liturgical prayers and hymns addressed Christ and the Holy Spirit directly, such as "Maranatha" ("Come, Lord Jesus") and "Veni Creator Spiritus" ("Come, Creator Spirit"). Even today, most hymns about the Holy Spirit are prayers to the Spirit (check the Pentecost section of nearly any Christian hymnal or songbook).

The Doctrine of the Trinity as Pastorally Significant

The early church debates were much more complex than this brief treatment can suggest. They featured intricate arguments regarding what precisely was "three" about God (what is a divine person?), what pre-

8. Athanasian Creed, verses 15 and 16.

9. See Robert Louis Wilken, *The Spirit of Early Christian Thought* (New Haven: Yale University Press, 2003), pp. 101-2, and Larry Hurtado, *Lord Jesus Christ: Devotion to Jesus in Earliest Christianity* (Grand Rapids: Eerdmans, 2003), pp. 137-53, 605-19.

cisely was "one" about God (what is the divine essence?), and what this meant for how the nature and identity of Jesus should be understood. Those discussions about the internal coherence of the doctrine continue to this day. But sometimes those discussions, important as they are, miss the vital pastoral implications of the doctrine and the significant ways that Trinity doctrine can ground and nurture the practice of worship.

A memorable sentence in Anne Lamott's memoir *Traveling Mercies* invites us to probe those pastoral dimensions. She says, "I had never stopped believing in God . . . [but] mine was a patchwork God, sewn together from bits of rag and ribbon, Eastern and Western, pagan and Hebrew, everything but the kitchen sink and Jesus."[10] All of us live with a "patchwork God," with our own limited understanding of God's being. Ours might be sewn together from children's Bible-story books or from old epic movies, from favorite hymns or Christmas cards, from Gallup polls or political debates. The inevitable result is some confusion about how to worship. Is our worship an act of obeisance, of currying divine favor, of nurturing warm sentimentality, or of expressing prophetic zeal? Should our worship arise out of gratitude and wonder, or out of guilt, fear, or shame?

In the context of these competing impulses, the doctrine of the Trinity is a clarifying, reassuring, and imagination-expanding resource. Consider three crucial pastoral corollaries.

First, the doctrine of the Trinity means that God is not different from what we see in Jesus. In Deist or Unitarian theology, Jesus Christ, while still viewed as a key teacher, a good person, and a remarkable prophet, is not viewed on a par with God. In contrast, the doctrine of the Trinity maintains the scandalous claim that Jesus Christ is perfectly divine. As such, Jesus is a faithful witness, a transparent window into divine life. "If you want to know who God is," says theologian William Placher, "attend to these stories about Jesus Christ," for Jesus is the "best clue to who God is." On this view, we need not fear that God is other than what we see in Christ. As Daniel Migliore concludes, "Classical Trinitarian doctrine . . . wants to say that there is no sinister or even de-

10. Anne Lamott, *Traveling Mercies* (New York: Pantheon Books, 1999), p. 41.

monic side of God altogether different from what we know in the story of Jesus who befriended the poor and forgave sinners. God *is* self-expanding, other-affirming, community-building love."[11]

Second, a Trinitarian doctrine of God sturdily reinforces our understanding of God's lavish grace or unmerited favor toward us. The New Testament teaches that Jesus and the Holy Spirit are agents of divine redemption. Their work accomplishes salvation for us and for the whole cosmos. They are the savior and advocate on whom we rely. From a Deist or Unitarian view, the exemplary human Jesus shows us the way but ultimately leaves us with a lot of work to do to save ourselves and the world around us. But from a Trinitarian view, in which Jesus Christ and the Holy Spirit are seen as not less than God, their actions can be trusted to be fully effective. The triune God not only models salvation but accomplishes it. This frees us to live in grateful obedience, free from the worry that somehow we need to add more to the work accomplished by Christ and the Spirit.

Third, the doctrine of the Trinity offers us the magnificent, counter-cultural claim that divine life consists most fundamentally in interpersonal communion. This One God in three Persons exists in relation to and for the other. At the heart of the universe is not the "will to power" (Nietzsche) but rather "Being-in-Communion" (Zizioulas).[12] In contrast to a Deist or Unitarian theology that tends to view divine life as one of pristine isolation, Trinitarian theology stresses that God's life is one of abundant communion, a kind of fellowship (or *koinonia*) that overflows to include us.

In sum, God is reliably known in Christ. Grace is sufficient. Communion abounds at the heart of the universe. These claims are so lovely, so musical, and so luminous that not even a lifetime of theological reflection can begin to exhaust them. No wonder Jonathan Edwards sim-

11. See William Placher, *Narratives of a Vulnerable God: Christ, Theology, and Scripture* (Louisville: Westminster/John Knox Press, 1984), p. 55; and Daniel Migliore, *Faith Seeking Understanding: An Introduction to Christian Theology* (Grand Rapids: Eerdmans, 1991), p. 63.

12. Friedrich Nietzsche, *The Will to Power*, trans. Walter Kaufmann and R. J. Hollingdale (New York: Vintage, 1968), and John Zizioulas, *Being as Communion: Studies in Personhood and the Church* (Crestwood, N.Y.: St. Vladimir's Seminary Press, 1985).

ply concluded, "God has appeared glorious to me on account of the Trinity."[13]

Making the Trinitarian Shape of Christian Worship Clear

Yet, this music often falls on deaf ears. Often the doctrine of the Trinity is dismissed as either obtuse or irrelevant. It is viewed as a mathematical puzzle to be solved rather than a pastoral resource for clearing our clouded imaginations. Millions of Christians, even those otherwise committed to orthodox, classical Christian teaching, have never been invited into the riches of Trinitarian worship, Trinitarian thinking, and Trinitarian living. This is like traveling to Banff but never leaving the hotel room to look at the Canadian Rockies!

Other Christians do practice Trinitarian worship, but without acknowledging or highlighting it. They sing hymns to God the Father, the Son, and the Spirit, but choose to remain perplexed at the oddity of the phrasing rather than explore its meaning. They teach their children to end their prayers with the words "in Jesus' name, Amen," but they are content to let this be merely a hasty phrase to wrap things up. Fortunately, the Trinitarian logic of worship is true even when we don't sing hymns to the Trinity or think much about Jesus' work in perfecting our worship and the Spirit's work in prompting it.

Still, we should not be content with this. The problem here is that often these Trinitarian practices remain attached to a way of conceiving of God that is functionally Deist. In our heart of hearts, we still think of God as remote, detached, or isolated. What a missed opportunity! Reflecting on the Trinitarian nature of our worship can help us grow into the fullness of biblical teaching about God, to let this splendid diamond of Christian theological reflection truly shine. Trinitarian worship and theological reflection are not a duty but a delight.

13. Jonathan Edwards, *Personal Narrative*, as cited in Amy Plantinga Pauw, *The Supreme Harmony of All: The Trinitarian Theology of Jonathan Edwards* (Grand Rapids: Eerdmans, 2002), p. 1.

Beginning Worship in a Trinitarian Way

Take four common actions that frequently comprise the opening of worship: congregating, inviting, praising, and praying. Each of these actions gains significance in light of the Trinitarian shape of worship, and can be practiced even more deeply when this Trinitarian logic is made clear.

Congregating

Worship begins with a grand processional, as people leave their homes, apartments, dorm rooms, nursing-home rooms, and hospital beds to walk, wheel, or drive to a gathering space. On one level, this is an altogether ordinary event. After all, basketball games, concerts, and lectures all feature such gathering.

But if we squint a bit, we can see this procession as a remarkable Trinitarian event. In this processional, people are gathering to address God, to engage with the One who created the cosmos. In this processional, people come because they are prompted by the Spirit. Perhaps the Holy Spirit will use an invitation of a friend or neighbor, perhaps a newspaper ad, perhaps even a sense of obligation or duty to draw the congregation together. In this processional, people from all sorts of backgrounds come to gather around the person of Jesus Christ. In many contexts, the congregation gathers around pulpit, font, and table, furniture that symbolizes how Christ comes to us. Congregating is an act of Spirit-forged coming together around the person of Christ for the purpose of addressing God. This Trinitarian geography is highlighted in the words of Delores Dufner:

> God, you call us to this place, where we know your love and grace.
> Here your hospitality makes of us one family,
> makes our rich diversity richer still in unity,
> makes our many voices one, joined in praise with Christ your Son.
>
> Now assembled in Christ's name, all your mercies to proclaim —
> in the hearing of your word, in our prayer through Christ the Lord,

in the ministries we share, learning how to serve with care —
in the Spirit let us be one in faith and unity.

In the water we were born of the Spirit in the Son.
Now a priestly, royal race rich in every gift of grace —
called, forgiven, loved, and freed, for the world we intercede:
gather into unity all the human family.[14]

Greeting and Call to Worship

The first words spoken in worship are crucial for establishing the purpose of the event, for making clear how the lines of communication in a worship service go. If the primary activity of the worship service is for worshipers to participate together in a gift-exchange of promises — by hearing God's Word, by offering prayers and praise, and by receiving the spiritual nourishment offered at the Lord's table — then the call to worship at its best reinforces both the "vertical dimension" of worship (that worship is an encounter between God and the gathered congregation) and the "horizontal dimension" of worship (because worship is fundamentally communal).

In many Christian traditions, the first words spoken convey God's invitation to worship (a call to worship) or announce God's active presence. This reinforces the theological assertion that God always comes to us before we come to God. Thus, it is

> God makes an eternal gift to the world of God's very self. Through the outpouring of God into our hearts as love, we become by grace what God is already by nature, namely, self-donating love for the other.
>
> Catherine Mowry LaCugna

14. Delores Dufner (b. 1939), "God, You Call Us to This Place," *Sing! A New Creation* (Grand Rapids: Faith Alive Publications, 2001), no. 14.

fitting for worship to begin with scriptural words that convey God's greeting to us (historically referred to in some traditions as the "salutation"). One of the most traditional texts for this purpose is also the most Trinitarian: "The grace of the Lord Jesus Christ, the love of God, and the communion of the Holy Spirit be with all of you" (2 Cor. 13:14). This is a simple, reassuring statement that we worship in the presence and through the working of the triune God.

Praise and Adoration

The primary response during the opening of worship is adoration. Many classic Christian songs and hymns of adoration are explicitly Trinitarian. "Holy, holy, holy . . . blessed Trinity!" we sing. Eastern Orthodox hymns of praise are pervasively Trinitarian. At their best, these hymns are not mindless expressions of correct theological jargon but rather thoughtful articulations that clear our thinking, that invite us to attend to the beauty and majesty of the God whose life is holy, loving communion.

It is important to remember that every act of praise is a strong act of negation as well as affirmation. Every time we sing praise to the triune God, we are asserting our opposition to anything that would attempt to stand in God's place. Every hymn of praise is a little anti-idolatry campaign, as Walter Brueggemann explains: "The affirmation of Yahweh always contains a polemic against someone else. . . . It may be that the [exiles] will sing such innocuous-sounding phrases as 'Glory to God in the highest,' or 'Praise God from whom all blessings flow.' Even those familiar phrases are polemical, however, and stake out new territory for the God now about to be aroused to new caring."[15] When we sing "Praise God, from whom all blessings flow," we are also saying "Down with the gods from whom no blessings flow."

15. Walter Brueggemann, *Cadences of Home: Preaching among the Exiles* (Louisville: Westminster/John Knox Press, 1997), p. 128. The polemic function of praise songs actually has close ties to Trinitarian theology. The body of Christian hymnody that is most polemic may well be the Trinitarian hymns of the fourth century, such as the *Te Deum* ("Holy God, We Praise Your Name") and "Of the Father's Love Begotten," which were weapons against Arianism.

Recognizing that our fleeting thoughts are elusive at best, when we sing in praise, our interior conversation may often go something like this (interior conversation in parentheses):

Praise God, from whom all blessings flow (yes, the stock market really has done well this week).

Praise Him, all creatures here below (though, come to think of it, we could be singing a little better if our praise team or organist would only go a little faster today).

Praise Him above, ye heavenly host (though it is difficult to maintain belief in angels in our secular culture).

Praise Father, Son, and Holy Ghost (what a nice, symmetrical way to end a song of praise). Amen.

What we need to recover is the experience of songs of praise — regardless of musical style — that function more like this:

Praise God, from whom all blessings flow (and not any lifeless idol, like the stock market or shopping mall!).

Praise Him, all creatures here below (because this God is far better than anything we could create from our own imaginations!).

Praise Him above, ye heavenly host (because even in heaven there is only One worthy of praise!).

Praise Father, Son, and Holy Ghost (because it is the triune God that both promises and effects life-giving redemption). Amen.[16]

---

16. The rhetorical device is adapted from Walter Brueggemann, *The Psalms and the Life of Faith*, ed. Patrick D. Miller (Minneapolis: Fortress Press, 1995), p. 127, and developed in a slightly different way in my article entitled "Isaiah in Christian Liturgy: Recovering Textual Contrasts and Correcting Theological Astigmatism," *Calvin Theological Journal* 39 (2004): 135-56.

For thoughtful, alert worshipers, there is nothing routine about singing praise to God.

Expectant Prayer

A fourth common element of the opening of worship is prayer. Most typically, this consists of a petition that God will work powerfully through the Spirit during the worship service. Many songs and hymns we sing as worship begins are, in fact, prayers. A particularly strong Trinitarian example comes from the tradition of Lutheran chorales:

> Lord Jesus Christ, be present now; our hearts in true devotion bow.
> Your Spirit send with light divine, and let your truth
>   within us shine.
>
> Unseal our lips to sing your praise in endless hymns
>   through all our days;
> increase our faith and light our minds; and set us free
>   from doubt that blinds.
>
> Then shall we join the hosts that cry, "O holy, holy Lord
>   Most High!"
> And in the light of that blest place we then shall see you
>   face to face.
>
> All glory to the Father, Son, and Holy Spirit, Three in One!
> To you, O blessed Trinity, be praise throughout eternity![17]

These petitions express both longing for God and deep dependence and humility. They acknowledge that the power in worship is a gift from God rather than a human accomplishment, and they explicitly confess that we approach God only through Christ in the power of the Spirit. This is a prayer that makes the Trinitarian grammar or logic of worship explicit.

---

17. "Lord Jesus Christ, Be Present Now," Wilhelm II (1598-1662), 1651, trans. Catherine Winkworth (1829-1878), *Lutheran Book of Worship* (Minneapolis: Augsburg Publishing House, 1978), no. 253.

Trinitarian Habits

The Trinitarian grammar or shape of worship is not confined to the beginning of a worship service. One helpful way of further exploring the Trinitarian logic of worship is to explore what we might call "Trinitarian worship habits." These are further traits or characteristics of worship practiced by communities that fully embrace Trinitarian ways of thinking and living. They are natural complements, corollaries, or consequences of fully embracing Trinitarian theology.[18] The following five habits are an illustrative — not an exhaustive — list of the liturgical habits of those whose theology is self-consciously Trinitarian.

Memory and Hope

First, Trinitarian worship is full of references to time — past, present, and future. One way of thinking about the controversy over the doctrine of the Trinity in the fourth and fifth centuries is to think of it as a controversy about how historical and concrete divine life could be. The doctrine of the Trinity makes a fundamental choice about how to speak about God's relationship to the world and to history. Arians and Deists of all times posit a god removed from history. Trinitarians posit a God who acts within history.

The liturgical corollary of this theme is simply that just as the Christian doctrine of God should be rooted in this history (often called "the divine economy"), so too Christian worship should rehearse the divine economy. God's actions in history are the basis for *both* the knowledge and the worship of the triune God. Christian liturgy is fundamentally an act of memory or *anamnesis,* an act of rehearsing God's actions in history: past and future, realized and promised. Christians identify the God they worship by naming God as the agent of particular actions in history.

18. Some of the most promising work on the doctrine of the Trinity focuses on its implications for various areas of Christian worship, doctrine, and life. See, for example, David Cunningham, *These Three Are One: The Practice of Trinitarian Theology* (Oxford: Blackwell, 1998).

This is a common theme in many definitions of worship. Thus, John Burkhardt argues that "true worship celebrates the most definite God of the covenant in Moses and Jesus, the God of Abraham, Isaac, and Jacob, of Sarah, Rebekah, and Rachel, and of countless others. Fundamentally, worship is the celebrative response to what God has done, is doing, and promises to do." And the 1993 *Book of Common Worship* concludes, "An important characteristic of worship in the Reformed tradition is that it centers on God rather than ourselves and our feelings. Our attention is drawn to the majesty and glory of the triune God, who created all things and by whose power all things are sustained, who was revealed in Jesus Christ raised from the dead to rule over all things, and who is at work as the giver of life in and among us by the power of the Holy Spirit."[19] On this view, worship is not primarily ahistorical, mystical introspection. Any Deist can praise God for timeless attributes; it takes a Trinitarian Christian to praise God for particular, concrete actions in history.[20]

Trinitarian Balance

Second, Trinitarian worship is also marked by balance. Richard Mouw wryly observes that "Christians play favorites with the members of the Trinity."[21] This is especially clear in worship. In some churches, references to the Holy Spirit outdistance references to Jesus or to God the Father by ten to one. In others, Jesus is nearly the exclusive focus. In still

19. See John Burkhardt, *Worship* (Philadelphia: Westminster Press, 1982), pp. 17, 6; and *The Book of Common Worship* (Louisville: Westminster/John Knox Press, 1993), p. 8.

20. Donald Bloesch, for example, links *ahistorical* mysticism with an attempt "to transcend the Trinity by positing a 'God above God,' an infinite abyss that lies beyond personality and diversity," which he identifies as "incontestably other than the God of Abraham, Isaac, and Jacob." See *The Struggle of Prayer* (San Francisco: Harper & Row, 1980), pp. 21, 27, and *God, the Almighty: Power, Wisdom, Holiness, Love* (Downers Grove, Ill.: InterVarsity Press, 1995), pp. 60, 176, 192, 231-34. This is not to say that contemplative prayer has no place in Christian worship, but rather that contemplation focused on biblical narratives and divine persons is more fitting to Trinitarian theology than personal introspection.

21. Richard Mouw, *The God Who Commands* (Notre Dame: University of Notre Dame Press, 1991), p. 150.

others, there are ample references to God but a kind of unexpressed embarrassment about the work of the Holy Spirit. Part of the value of the doctrine of the Trinity, as Richard Niebuhr observed, is that it serves as "a formulation of the *whole* Church's faith in God in distinction from the partial faiths and partial formulations of parts of the Church and of individuals in the Church." The doctrine is valuable "to correct the overemphases and partialities of the members of the whole not by means of a new over-emphasis but by means of a synthesized formula in which all the partial insights and convictions are combined."[22] Without a sense of overall balance, we are likely to think only about our favorite few biblical texts and themes. We are likely to miss the forest for the trees.

How is this Trinitarian balance reflected? It is primarily reflected over time, through the unfolding of perhaps a year's worth of worship services, as Scripture readings, sermons, hymns, and prayers focus on different aspects of the Bible and different aspects of God's work.

It can also be cultivated directly by inviting congregations to reflect explicitly on the work of each divine person. This was the obvious goal of sixteenth-century Puritan theologian John Owen, whose treatise on the Trinity features the characteristically long and self-explanatory title: *Of Communion with God the Father, Son, and Holy Ghost, Each Person Distinctly, in Love, Grace and Consolation.*

But this balance can also be tightly compressed in the space of a short prayer or hymn. It is perhaps most obvious in Trinitarian hymns that assign one stanza to each of the three divine persons, a form particularly developed by Charles Wesley and practiced by many hymnwriters throughout the church's history. Wesley penned dozens of Trinitarian hymns, including this one, sung to this day:

> Maker, in whom we live, in whom we are and move,
> the glory, power, and praise receive for thy creating love.
> Let all the angel throng give thanks to God on high,
> while earth repeats the joyful song and echoes to the sky.

22. H. Richard Niebuhr, "The Doctrine of the Trinity and the Unity of the Church," *Theology Today* 3 (1946): 372, 383.

Incarnate Deity, let all the ransomed race render in thanks
their lives to thee for thy redeeming grace.
The grace to sinners showed ye heavenly choirs proclaim, and cry,
"Salvation to our God, salvation to the Lamb!"

Spirit of Holiness, let all thy saints adore thy sacred energy,
and bless thine heart-renewing power.
Not angel tongues can tell thy love's ecstatic height,
the glorious joy unspeakable, the beatific sight.

Eternal, Triune God, let all the hosts above,
let all on earth below record and dwell upon thy love.
When heaven and earth are fled before thy glorious face,
sing all the saints thy love hath made thine everlasting praise.[23]

This Trinitarian pattern is also evident in many Eucharistic or Lord's Supper prayers, which begin with praise to the triune God, continue with explicit remembrance of Jesus' life, and conclude with an epicletic prayer for the Holy Spirit to work through the celebration.[24]

Trinitarian Integration

Third, Trinitarian worship seeks not only a balance of themes but also an integrated way of thinking that sees the Trinitarian dimensions of each individual topic, theme, or event.

Take Christmas, for example. Our Christmas cards, crèches, and storybooks are filled with the characters of the Christmas drama: Elizabeth, Zechariah, Mary, Joseph, the baby Jesus, angels, shepherds, magi, even Simeon and Anna. But the biblical account of Jesus' birth in the opening chapters of Matthew and Luke refers repeatedly to another par-

23. Charles Wesley, "Maker, in Whom We Live" (1707-1788), 1747, *United Methodist Hymnal* (Nashville: United Methodist Publishing House, 1989), no. 88.

24. Allan Bouley observes that this Trinitarian pattern emerged in tandem with early church reflections on Trinitarian theology. See *From Freedom to Formula: The Evolution of the Eucharistic Prayer from Oral Improvisation to Written Texts* (Washington, D.C.: Catholic University of America Press, 1981), p. 250.

ticipant in the Christmas drama: the Holy Spirit. Though often unnoticed and uncelebrated, it is the Holy Spirit who comes upon Mary, Elizabeth, Zechariah, and Simeon. Similarly, the Old Testament prophecies that foretell the inbreaking of God's kingdom frequently speak of the coming of the Spirit of the Lord, though these texts are strikingly underrepresented in most Advent worship services. The Holy Spirit is the forgotten participant in the Christmas drama. This omission is not only seen in the Christmas card selection at Hallmark but also heard in music for the season. There are dozens of shepherd carols, magi carols, angel carols, and Mary and Joseph carols, but precious few that acknowledge the work of the Spirit.

The juxtaposition of "Christmas" and "Holy Spirit" challenges our understanding of each. First, it anchors our understanding of the Spirit's work in the person of Jesus Christ: the Holy Spirit is not just any spirit we feel; it is the Spirit of Jesus Christ. "By this you know the Spirit of God: every spirit that confesses that Jesus Christ has come in the flesh is from God" (1 John 4:2). Second, it makes our understanding of Christmas more dynamic and personal: the same Spirit that came upon Mary, the same Spirit that anointed Jesus to preach good news to the poor and raised him from the dead, has now been poured into *our* hearts (Rom. 5:5). The same God who sent the Spirit to answer the waiting people of Israel is at work restoring creation and giving us hope. The Spirit makes *us* participants in the Christmas drama. It is true that some theologians have called the Holy Spirit "the shy member of the Trinity," because the Spirit always points us to Christ. Still, the biblical witness is clear in explicitly identifying the work of the Spirit, in part to reassure us that our

> To speak of God as triune is to set all of our prior understandings of what is divine in question. God is not a solitary monad but free, self-communicating love. God is not the supreme will-to-power over others but the supreme will-to-community in which power and life are shared. God consists not in dominating others but in sharing life with others.
>
> Daniel Migliore

recognition of Christ, our coming to faith, and our sharing in Christ's anointing is not something dependent on our own striving but rather is something we receive as a gift.

This integrated, Trinitarian view of Christmas is an example of a whole pattern of thinking that can inform and deepen our worship.

Correcting Theological Astigmatism

Fourth, Trinitarian worship is eager to correct misperceptions about God's character. If theologians who work on the doctrine of God are like ophthalmologists eager to correct the church's theological astigmatism, Trinitarian worship leaders, preachers, musicians, and artists are like optometrists who fit the glasses to the church's eyes to make the correction effective for ordinary churchgoers.

We've already seen how Trinitarian theology corrects our view of God as remote and isolated and replaces it with a view of God as relational. But this is just the beginning. As Daniel Migliore suggests, "Our reflections on the triune reality of God point to the need for a thorough rethinking of the doctrine of the attributes of God, which have all too often been presented and debated without any reference to the life, death, and resurrection of Jesus Christ or to the doctrine of the Trinity."[25] When we theologize and worship in a Trinitarian way, we take care to explore how each topic of our reflection is challenged and deepened by approaching it from the whole range of biblical texts and from the perspective of each divine person.

Migliore himself illustrates this process in his reflection on the nature of divine power. He argues, "The doctrine of the Trinity represents a revolution in the understanding of the power of God. . . . Christians do not worship absolute power."[26] Christians do not understand God's power to be "sheer almightiness." God is not like a divine Rambo. Rather, God's power can best be understood through the story of Jesus Christ, through the Incarnation, where God takes on human form, becomes one

25. Migliore, *Faith Seeking Understanding*, p. 72.
26. Daniel Migliore, *The Power of God* (Philadelphia: Westminster Press, 1983), p. 77.

of us, and accepts all the limitations of humanity, sin excepted. Trinitarian power, as revealed in Jesus' prayer to his Father in John 17, looks a lot like mutuality and reciprocity, like intimate divine cooperation. The power of God is shared power, a rather stark contrast to the world's power that controls and hoards. God's power shares, protects, and gives up for the other. God's power seeks justice and fellowship. The doctrine of the Trinity does not call into question the capacity of God's power. It does focus our attention on the fact that God's power is aimed at certain purposes and exercised in particular ways. It helps us re-interpret our understanding of what power is and how, then, we should shape our communities in ways that mirror God's own Trinitarian community.

David Willis adds a crucial reminder at this point. As important as it is to note that a biblical portrayal of Trinitarian power points away from sheer brute strength and might and toward self-giving love and mutuality, it is equally important to guard against a "romanticizing of powerlessness."[27]

In recent years several theologians have joined Migliore in this work of correcting misperceptions of God's character by bringing the best biblical and theological tools to bear, guided by a biblical, Trinitarian grammar. Misperceptions vary in different church contexts. Some contexts are plagued by the notion of God as an impersonal, distant deity and a corresponding notion of worship as detached, disinterested, aloof contemplation. In other contexts, God is perceived as fearsome, tyrannical, or despotic, and worship becomes fearful obeisance. In still other communities, God is presented as a cosmic accountant, keeping careful records of credits and debits; worship, on this dreary view, is merely an act of paying dues. Yet another theological misperception is a view of God that is especially schmaltzy or sentimental, a liturgical worry especially near Christmas.

A Trinitarian correction of theological astigmatism brings wonderful clarity of vision into worship through the work of preachers, liturgists, hymnwriters, and artists. Consider this poignant Advent hymn adapted by Scottish hymnwriter John Bell:

27. David Willis, *Notes on the Holiness of God* (Grand Rapids: Eerdmans, 2002), p. 15.

Lift up your heads, eternal gates, Alleluia!
See how the King of glory waits, Alleluia!
The Lord of Hosts is drawing near,
the Savior of the world is here. Alleluia!

But not in arms or battle dress, Alleluia!
God comes, a child, amidst distress, Alleluia!
No mighty armies shield the way,
only coarse linen, wool, and hay. Alleluia!

God brings a new face to the brave, Alleluia!
God redefines who best can save: Alleluia!
not those whose power relies on threat,
terror or torture, destruction or debt. Alleluia!

God's matchless and majestic strength, Alleluia!
in all its height, depth, breadth, and length, Alleluia!
now is revealed, its power to prove,
by Christ protesting, "God is love!" Alleluia![28]

Bell's work cannot be sung on automatic pilot. It artfully but prophetically challenges us to rethink our implicit understanding of God's character.

Communion

Finally, Trinitarian worship is marked by joyful attention to the rich experience of communion that is at the heart of both God's triune life and the Christian life. "May they be one as we are one," Jesus prayed (John 17:22). Reflexively, John announced, "Truly our fellowship is with the Fa-

28. John Bell, "Lift Up Your Heads," Choral Octavo G-5494 (Chicago: GIA Publications, Inc., 2002), text copyright © 2001 Wild Goose Resource Group, Iona Community. All rights reserved. Used by permission of GIA Publications, Inc., Chicago, exclusive North American agent. Original text: "Lift Up Your Heads, Ye Mighty Gates," written by George Weissel (1590-1635), 1642, translated by Catherine Winkworth (1827-1878), 1855; adapted by John Bell (b. 1949), 2002.

ther and with his Son Jesus Christ" (1 John 1:3). This is a vision which accentuates fellowship or *koinonia* as a primary attribute of divine life, and which contends that human communal life should model, embody, and mirror that deep communion. This vision draws on the metaphor of *perichoresis* or "indwelling" — an "in-ness" relationship first intimated in the Gospel of John, which envisions divine life as a dynamic dance in which God's unity is a function of active relations.

When seen as a vision for human life, this attention to communion protests against any forms of ecclesiastical or societal individualism. In the words of Lesslie Newbigin, "The Church is called to be a union of [those] with Christ in the love of the Father whereby their separate beings are made one with that perfect mutual interpenetration in love, that perfect community which is the glory of God."[29] To use a phrase of seventeenth-century theologian Richard Sibbes, "The trinity should be the pattern of our unity."[30]

It is not hard to see the implications here for Christian worship. Christian worship is one arena where a Trinitarian vision for the church is most tangibly expressed. Worship reflects, embodies, and enacts a rich tapestry of relationships. Like concentric circles, the relationships flow out first from those between Jesus and the Father in the Spirit, then to the relationships between the triune God and God's people, and then to the relationships between the members of Christ's Body through our life in the Spirit. At its best, Christian liturgy embodies the mutuality and *koinonia* of a Trinitarian ecclesiology. At its best, it enacts and prefigures the kingdom of God. In a public, concrete way, Christian worship is an icon or window of our union with Christ through the work of the Holy Spirit. In a public, concrete way, Christian worship is an icon or window into the web of relationships that make up the Christian church. Communion-oriented worship is a vision that some congregations express regularly in worship as they sing songs like this one:

29. Lesslie Newbigin, *The Household of God* (Cincinnati: Friendship Press, 1953), p. 140.
30. Richard Sibbes, *Complete Works*, vol. 3, p. 194, quoted in Pauw, *The Supreme Harmony of All*, p. 35.

God, the Father of your people, you have called us to be one;
grant us grace to walk together in the joy of Christ, your Son.
Challenged by your Word and Spirit, blest with gifts
      from heaven above,
as one body we will serve you and bear witness to your love.

May the grace of Christ, our Savior, and the Father's boundless love,
with the Holy Spirit's favor, rest upon us from above.
May we now remain in union with each other and the Lord,
and possess, in sweet communion, joys that earth cannot afford.[31]

Public worship embodies this vision any time worshipers are invited
from isolation to fellowship, from coercion to reciprocity, from self-
centeredness to self-giving. Communion within the church might be
realized in practice in many complementary ways: through architecture
that emphasizes human relationality, through greater inclusion of persons with disabilities, and through servant-oriented views of Christian
leadership. It might be realized practically in sermons that aim at restoration of community, in truly common prayers that express the concerns of all members of the community, and in corporate almsgiving as
an action of Christian love. It might be seen in the collaborative creation
of liturgical art-forms, in the sharing of songs and prayers across cultures and traditions, in language that is Trinitarian and accessible, and in
worship practices that are fully intergenerational. This vision of perfect
communion is never fully realized this side of heaven, of course. But
worship is one place where we dare to name this vision and actively anticipate the day in which it will be fully realized.[32]

In sum, these liturgical practices — reciting history, maintaining
balance, thinking and worshiping with an integrated theological vision,
correcting theological astigmatism, and embodying communion — are

31. "God, the Father of Your People," stanza 1, Alfred E. Mulder (b. 1936), 1978, stanza
2, John Newton (1725-1807), 1779, *Psalter Hymnal* (Grand Rapids: CRC Publications, 1987),
no. 322. Stanza 1, copyright © 1987 CRC Publications, Grand Rapids, MI, 1-800-333-8300.
Used by permission.
32. See the chapter "Eucharist" below.

natural habits of those who attend to God's triune character. Amy Plantinga Pauw has observed that Jonathan Edwards wrote extensively on the doctrine of the Trinity but rarely preached about it. She concludes that his Trinitarian theology functioned like "a subterranean river" throughout his ministry, shaping his theological imagination and his ministerial instincts.[33] Likewise, these liturgical habits emerge out of being rooted in classical Christian theology, and they function to keep Christian communities grounded in the gospel of grace through Christ.

Trinitarian Criteria

These Trinitarian habits can also be rephrased as criteria for Christian worship. In a time of remarkable liturgical change, it is tempting to focus many of our discussions about worship on styles of preaching, music, or art. The challenge for leaders is to address deeper issues, to ground our worship in a biblical vision of God. The way to do this is to make irreducibly theological conversation an active part of our planning and evaluating worship. Leaders actively seeking to practice Trinitarian worship might ask questions like these:

1. Does our liturgy speak of God with reference to particular actions in history recorded in Scripture?
2. Does corporate worship in our congregation rehearse the whole of the divine economy in a balanced way?
3. Does worship present each particular biblical event and image in an integrated way, with attention to how it fits in the whole framework of biblical teaching and the triune work of God?
4. Does worship open up the meaning of these events in ways that help us perceive God's character more clearly, correcting the theological astigmatism to which we are prone?
5. Does the community itself model the kind of intimate fellowship or *koinonia* that is central to both divine life and the Christian life, and

33. Pauw, *The Supreme Harmony of All*, p. 3.

do we see the Trinity's own communion as the source of that communion?

One strength of these criteria is that they are applicable not only in specific cultural settings. These criteria have as much to say about corporate worship offered in a Central American barrio or in the African bush as in a wealthy, suburban congregation in North America or in a majestic European cathedral. They are as applicable to a worship service offered at a summer camp or to a mission congregation as to a denominational assembly or to a gathering of the North American Academy of Liturgy. They are the kind of questions that apply to contextual ministry in any setting.

> Almighty God, you have revealed to your Church your eternal Being of glorious majesty and perfect love as one God in Trinity of Persons: Give us grace to continue steadfast in the confession of this faith, and constant in our worship of you, Father, Son, and Holy Spirit; for you live and reign, one God, now and for ever. Amen.
>
> Trinity collect from the
> *Book of Common Prayer*

Another virtue of these criteria is that they are *theological*. They emerge not only out of historical study or aesthetic preference, but also out of reflection on the mystery of the gospel that Christians proclaim. Long-term worship renewal doesn't come out of singing a little faster, praying a little harder, or making worship a bit more proper or a bit more fun. Worship renewal can issue only from the depth and mystery of the gospel that Christians proclaim. Christian worship is strongest when it is integrally and self-consciously related to the person and work of Jesus Christ and the power of the Holy Spirit. The study of Christian worship is most helpful to Christian communities when it demonstrates how this has happened in the past and how it might happen in the future in more profound ways.

Finally, the value of Trinitarian reflection on worship is the compelling picture it paints of the God Christians worship, the community that offers this worship, and the actions used to do so. This vision invites preachers, artists, hymnwriters, musicians, liturgists, and poets to create art works, music, and texts that express "a more profound Alleluia." This vision invites liturgists and pastors to plan and lead worship that portrays the privilege of Christian corporate worship, and to teach and nurture their congregations regarding what this privilege is all about. And this vision compellingly invites worshipers to experience the grace of a self-giving God and to join with all the faithful of every time and place who forever sing to the glory of God's name.

Come, Great God of All the Ages

Come, great God of all the ages,
make your earthly mission known;
speak through every deed and person,
let your way and will be shown.
Guide the church to true commitment,
give direction, now, we ask;
fit us for the work of building,
dedicate us to the task.

Come, Christ Jesus, flesh and spirit,
sure foundation, cornerstone;
help us form the church eternal,
may your vision be our own.
Send a message to each follower,
lead all people to your way;
urge us to strong faith and action
as we build the church today.

Come, great Spirit, in and with us,
tune our ears to hear your call;
through the moving of your presence,
let redeeming love recall
ministry in dedication,
love embodied in our deeds;
challenge us to do your bidding,
see your purpose, fill all needs.

Come, O come, in celebration,
household of the one true God;
in commitment and rejoicing
let us go where Christ has trod.
As we act in faith and reverence,
let us, Lord, the future see;
place us in the church triumphant,
now and for eternity.

Mary Jackson Cathey (b. 1926), 1987

God the Spirit, Guide and Guardian

God the Spirit, guide and guardian,
windsped flame and hovering dove,
breath of life and voice of prophets,
sign of blessing, power of love:
give to those who lead your people
fresh anointing of your grace;
send them forth as bold apostles
to your church in every place.

Christ our Savior, Sovereign, Shepherd,
Word made flesh, Love crucified,
teacher, healer, suffering Servant,
friend of sinners, foe of pride:
in your tending may all pastors*
learn and live a Shepherd's care;
grant them courage and compassion
shown through word and deed and prayer.

Great Creator, Life-bestower,
Truth beyond all thought's recall,
fount of wisdom, womb of mercy,
giving and forgiving all:
as you know our strength and weakness,
so may those the church exalts
oversee her life steadfastly,
yet not overlook her faults.

Triune God, mysterious Being,
undivided and diverse,
deeper than our minds can fathom,
greater than our creeds rehearse:
help us in our varied callings
your full image to proclaim,
that our ministries uniting
may give glory to your name.

Carl P. Daw Jr. (b. 1944), 1988

*"elders" or "deacons"

Confession and Assurance | Sin and Grace

William A. Dyrness

During a visit to a flea market near her home, writer Anne Lamott tells of hearing wonderful music coming from a church across the street. Before long, she says, "I began stopping in at St. Andrew from time to time, standing in the doorway to listen to the songs." She returned about once a month but was grateful no one tried to persuade her to stay or even to sit down. She always left before the sermon. Only after several months of visits did she take a seat in one of the folding chairs along the back, letting the music envelop her. She describes what happened then: "Something inside that was stiff and rotting would feel soft and tender. . . . Sitting there, standing with them to sing, sometimes so shaky and sick that I felt like I might tip over, I felt bigger than myself, like I was being taken care of, tricked into coming back to life."[1]

In this chapter we consider that part of the worship service in which the congregation is called, invited to confess their sins before God and then to receive God's declaration of forgiveness. In most services, this is a part of the gathering for worship. Before the Word is read and proclaimed, the people together acknowledge the reality of sin in their personal and common life. After their corporate confession, frequently a time of silence follows for personal prayers of confession. Then the pastor or liturgist speaks words of assurance. "As far as the east is from the west, so far God removes our transgressions from us" is one biblical as-

1. Anne Lamott, *Traveling Mercies* (New York: Pantheon, 1999), pp. 46, 48.

surance of pardon from Psalm 103. The theological themes of sin and grace that inform the liturgical events of the confession of sin and the assurance of pardon will be explored here.

Anne Lamott's experience of "worship reluctance" may fairly be taken as a paradigm of the problem we have with worship: True worship does not come naturally to us. There are many things that keep us from worship — either from coming to church at all, or, having been persuaded to come, from actually engaging in genuine worship. Our natural inclination, in fact, is to stand in the back of the church, or indeed to stand outside the church altogether. We might feel that we are not good enough to worship a holy God, or we might be overwhelmed with the painful failures that have bedeviled us during the previous week. Or perhaps we feel too good to go in and sit down, feeling in some way that we don't need what the church has to offer. Or, on occasion, we might feel we would not be welcome, or that we would not feel at home in church — the songs and rituals and vocabulary all seem strange to us. Sometimes, like Lamott, we may simply feel too broken, "rotten," or hurt to make the effort.

Worship does not come naturally to us, fundamentally, because we are sinners. All of our relationships — with God, with each other, and with creation — are damaged. Shalom, God's original intent for us, has been destroyed. The meaning of the confession of sin and the assurance of pardon is very profound: it is the place in worship where shalom between God and people is restored. Christ has reconciled the believer to God and opened the way for us to worship "in spirit and in truth" (John 4:24). In addition, shalom between people can take genuine steps forward in the prayer of confession. When the congregation together prays "Lord, have mercy," and when each individual silently prays "Create in me a clean heart, O God," the Spirit of God finds new paths for reconciliation and joy. In some congregations, the confession of sin and the assurance of pardon have dropped out of worship liturgies because worship planners have judged them to be "depressing." This is a sad misunderstanding of their true function in worship. The confession and the assurance are, in reality, a celebration of the identity of the congregation as a community of the baptized. The congregation has, once again, affirmed the reconciliation that is their reality, heard the words from God that promise them this, and then stood with all their brothers and sisters in Christ to rejoice together in the grace that makes this relationship with God possible.

Sin as an Obstacle to Worship

Baptist preacher Will Campbell summarized the Christian faith in just nine words. He said, "We're no damn good, but God loves us anyway."[2] Confession is necessary, quite simply, because we are sinners. This is the ground and starting point of any true understanding of worship. When asked why we do not feel like worshiping God, our natural response is to point to someone else's failure: the minister's, or some Christian we once knew. We do not usually connect this with any failure on our part. Of course, the reasons connected with the failure of others are often compelling. But this does not negate the fact that underneath all this, the worship of a holy God is not natural to them or to us; we normally do not feel we need or want to worship God.

At least that is what we tell ourselves. It is true: we are all too familiar with issues of broken relationships and personal failures, and the shame that often results. When we are alone with ourselves, we know what we are like. And we have a deep longing to be accepted unconditionally. This is captured movingly in this short poem written by a teenage girl:

Don't criticize.
Don't analyze.
Don't even try to sympathize.
Don't say you understand because you don't.
Just hold me in your arms for once.
And love me as I am.

Like my mommy used to do
Before the world grew up on me.[3]

2. Will D. Campbell, *Brother to a Dragonfly* (New York: Continuum, 1994), p. 220.
3. Quoted in John Fischer, "Praise for the Unrenowned," *CCM* (*Contemporary Christian Music Magazine*), vol. 20, no. 4 (October 1997): 94.

Everyone in one way or another recognizes feelings like this. Our problem is that we do not ordinarily connect our feelings of inadequacy or loneliness with God, or with our estrangement from God. We often do not even connect them with any failure or mistake on our part. All of this, which the biblical witnesses connect with "sin," is simply not recognized. So in various ways we seek to avoid facing our failures — confession is not a natural practice. Indeed, it makes little sense outside the Christian context of sin and grace.

Biblical Context

It is important for us then to begin with a clear understanding of the biblical teaching about sin and the ways this has been interpreted in the Christian tradition. In the beginning, the Genesis account notes, the man and woman had a natural relationship with God. The whole of life was lived in God's presence; in a sense, all of life was a kind of hymn or dance of worship, an active enjoyment of the presence of God. Unfortunately, Adam and Eve did not acknowledge the limits that were natural to creation and denied God's goodness by disobeying God's instructions. The whole of Genesis depicts the disruption and oppression that their hubris cost them. It necessitated God's delivering work in Exodus and the giving of the law at Sinai.

The Old Testament has many ways of describing the results of human rebellion against God, each of them shedding different light on the barriers to worship we have noted. There are several Hebrew words for sin which refer to the various ways that we "miss the way God intended" (hattâh) for us in the law, a word that literally means "instruction." Two other Hebrew words for sin stress the deliberate human act of defiance (pesha and âwôn). A range of others refer to the puzzling persistence of sin that seems built into us.[4]

The Old Testament stresses that we are guilty before God, that we

---

4. See the discussion of "Sin, sinners," in the *Interpreter's Dictionary of the Bible* (Nashville: Abingdon, 1962), vol. 4, pp. 361-67.

deserve punishment, and that some sacrifice must be made to cover our sins. For sin has finally to do with God and God's holiness, and so something must be done to repair the gulf our sin has caused. When you realize your guilt, the Old Testament says, you must confess the sin, "and you shall bring to the LORD . . . a sin offering; and the priest shall make atonement on your behalf for your sin" (Lev. 5:5-6).

The New Testament picks up the basic teaching of the Old Testament about sin and connects it directly to the work that Christ accomplished in his death and resurrection. Sin is still a deviation from what is good, a transgression of the law that constitutes wrongdoing and makes one guilty (hamartia). In the end it is "an offence in relation to God with emphasis on guilt."[5] Christ's death is variously pictured as the offering for sin (Rom. 3:25), as a great exchange (2 Cor. 5:21), and as a deliverance of the believer from evil powers (Col. 2:14-15), among other New Testament images of salvation. All these rich biblical images proclaim that Christ, through his life, death, and resurrection, has initiated a new era in which sin and death have been decisively defeated and righteousness has been established.

> The biggest biblical idea about sin, expressed in a riot of images and terms, is that sin is an anomaly, an intruder, a notorious gatecrasher. Sin does not belong in God's world, but somehow it has gotten in. In fact, sin has dug in, and, like a tick, burrows deeper when we try to remove it.
>
> Cornelius Plantinga Jr.

As a result of this decisive intervention of God, which the Exodus event anticipated in the Old Testament, the issue is no longer that of meeting the demands of the law but that of faith in Christ. In the New Testament this is represented and appropriated by baptism into Christ's death (Rom. 6:1-4). By this baptism we bear witness to the fact that God has "rescued us from the power of darkness, and transferred us into the

---

5. *Theological Dictionary of the New Testament*, vol. 1, ed. G. Kittel, trans. Geoffrey W. Bromiley (Grand Rapids: Eerdmans, 1964), p. 295.

kingdom of his beloved Son, in whom we have redemption, the forgiveness of sins" (Col. 1:13-14).

Of course, even Christians, though dwelling in Christ by the power of the Holy Spirit, will continue to sin, and therefore must continually pray "Forgive us our sins" (Luke 11:4). The victory over sin and evil has been won, but we live in what has been called by some theologians the "already" and the "not yet," the time in which Christ's victory is guaranteed but not yet fully visible.[6] The practice of confession, then, is a continuing recognition that by our own strength we are unable to come before God in worship. The prayer of confession is both an acknowledgment of sin as well as a recognition of the grace of God that has already been expressed in Christ's death, and the victory over sin that has already been achieved through his death and resurrection. In the prayer of confession, we acknowledge both our guilt and our gratitude at one and the same time. We are both humble in our recognition that we do not deserve to be in the presence of almighty God and yet deeply at home with our loving Father. The prayer of confession is, in many ways, a deep mystery. It strikes at the heart of what Frederick Buechner calls the "tragedy, comedy, and fairy tale" of the gospel. The Christian faith is a startling and completely unexpected blend of the darkness of the world (the tragedy), the unexpected joy of God's grace (the comedy), and the astonishing story of the gospel (the fairy tale). Worship touches each of these moments: the tragedy is expressed in the prayer of confession itself, the comedy in the assurance of pardon, and the fairy tale in the whole sweep of the worship service, focused especially in the proclamation of the word in sermon and sacrament.

Historical Developments in the Doctrine of Sin

The Christian tradition has been decisively influenced by Augustine, who defined sin in terms of both pride and desire. The Roman Catholic

---

6. For a good summary of this view, also called "realized eschatology," see Anthony Hoekema, *The Bible and the Future* (Grand Rapids: Eerdmans, 1979), pp. 15-22.

tradition has stressed desire, or concupiscence, while the Protestant traditions, in general, have focused more on pride as the basic expression of sin. John Calvin said that, though God created us with an original nobility, we have turned this into self-seeking pride, manifested in a refusal to submit ourselves to God. He says that "since blind self-love is innate in all mortals, they are most freely persuaded that nothing inheres in themselves that deserves to be considered hateful."[7] Simply put, we are blind to our own faults. As the biblical writer put it, "If we say that we have no sin, we deceive ourselves, and the truth is not in us" (1 John 1:8). The truth is that, as Augustine saw, all human projects are infected with the perversion caused by an exalted human pride and a distorted will.

This distorted will or misplaced desire has been developed more fully in the Catholic tradition. Just as pride in itself is not evil, so desire for Catholics is not in itself wrong. Sin derives from placing a desire for some temporal good above the desire for the supreme good, which is God. Sin, as Thomas Aquinas said, is "the inordinate longing for some temporal good" that is grounded in the "the inordinate love of self."[8] In the Catholic view, God imparts grace that leads a person to desire goods that lead ultimately to God. Since God is the natural end of humanity, sin can also be defined in terms of voluntary acts against the natural order that God has created. As Dutch Catholic theologian Piet Schoonenberg put it, "The sinful person acts against his or her being or against their neighbor's being."[9] This notion has been developed in ecumenical circles recently in terms of actions that disrupt not only human community but also the goodness and ecological order of creation.

Contemporary discussions of sin tend to focus more holistically on the broken relationships in which sin manifests itself. Karl Barth, for example, understood sin in terms of pride but also as sloth and falsehood.[10] All three sins can be understood in their capacities to under-

7. John Calvin, *Institutes of the Christian Religion*, ed. John T. McNeill, trans. Ford Lewis Battles (Philadelphia: Westminster Press, 1960), 2.1.2.

8. Thomas Aquinas, *Summa Theologica* I-II, q.77, a.4.

9. Schoonenberg, in *Theological Encyclopedia: The Concise Sacramentum Mundi*, ed. Karl Rahner (New York: Seabury, 1975), p. 1581.

10. Cf. Karl Barth, *Church Dogmatics* (Edinburgh: T&T Clark, 1957), IV.1-3.

mine and destroy relationships.[11] Similarly, Reinhold Niebuhr took a holistic view of sin by focusing on the ambiguity and paradox of human existence. He noted the complexity of all human decisions and their inevitable violation of the law of love. Contemporary Christian feminists, too, take a more relational perspective to the theology of sin. Sin is understood as whatever opposes God's will for our flourishing; whatever "gets in the way" of what God originally created us to be — persons living together in right and proper relationships — is sin.[12]

These broader perspectives allow theologians to focus not only on discrete personal sins but also on social sins and structural sins, not only on doing what is wrong but also on failing to do what is right. Sin in all its multiple and insidious forms not only infects our individual lives but also disrupts community, deforms institutions, and even damages the creation itself.

Thus, recent discussions of sin, without denying the element of personal choice, have emphasized that sin has important social and ecological consequences. This broader awareness has led to a new complexity in our understanding of sin. Here we might mention three elements that contribute to this complexity. A corporate awareness of sin has led to a new recognition of sin as *pollution*. This, of course, connects with parts of the Christian tradition and with contemporary settings where these themes have been dominant. As far back as the time of Augustine, there were those who focused not primarily on pride and subsequent guilt but on pollution and shame. The Montanists insisted that sin brought actual impurity that made it impossible for a minister guilty of a moral lapse to administer the sacraments. Thus, as David stressed in Psalm 51, forgiveness needed to involve real cleansing and restoration. Frequently, throughout Christian history, the focus on objective guilt and forgive-

---

11. Contemporary discussions of the old medieval list of "the seven deadly sins" (gluttony, pride, sloth, anger, envy, lust, and greed) have helpfully pointed out that the sin of "sloth" is not as simple as laziness and is *not* the same as the terrible lethargy of depression. Clinical depression is not sin; it is a treatable illness. The sin of sloth is a deliberate turning away from the gifts of God.

12. Serene Jones, "Human Beings as Sinners against God," in *Essentials of Christian Theology*, ed. W. Placher (Louisville: Westminster Press, 2003), p. 149.

ness has given sin a forensic character that obscures the elements of impurity and shame. An exception arises with African Christians, who are heirs of the cultural traditions represented by the Montanists. Notions of pollution are deeply imbedded in their traditions, and as a result, they have resonated with these overlooked biblical emphases.

Second, a broader understanding of sin as *brokenness* can make us sensitive to the suffering we all share because of sin. Again, Scripture recognizes that sin is much more than personal transgression, that sin also includes social, structural, and ecological brokenness, and it invites us to bring our multiple and painful experiences of brokenness into the very center of our worship of God. Recently, this awareness has led to a recovery of biblical lament as a critical component of worship, one that facilitates the turn to hope. As the Psalmist knew, God hears our cries of grief and protest. Without these cries, Kathleen Billman and Daniel Migliore argue, "there is no recognition of the real bondage and alienation of present reality . . . no genuine cry for deliverance, and no openness for new acts of God's grace."[13] An acknowledgment of the connection between sin and brokenness and subsequent suffering allows us to recognize lament, both inside and outside of the church, as theologically related to the Christian notion of confession.

Third, this larger conception of sin has made us sensitive to our misperceptions of ourselves and of others. Among certain groups of people, especially women and minorities, sin takes the insidious form of *self-deprecation*. Many people living on the margins or in places of powerlessness in society not only are forced to suffer humiliation or discrimination by those in power, but are made complicit in the process. As Justo Gonzáles points out, these marginalized people are often tempted to deny not only their rights but also the gifts they have to offer. They are taught that any form of resistance is wrong. Many "refuse to face up to a difficult struggle by convincing themselves that they are indeed to be

---

13. Kathleen D. Billman and Daniel L. Migliore, *Rachel's Cry: Prayer of Lament and Rebirth of Hope* (Cleveland: United Church Press, 1999), p. 126. They point out how lament has been progressively eliminated from our prayer books and make a strong case for its recovery.

subservient, that to refuse to claim their own identity is a virtue."[14] These suffer twice: first by being belittled and then by being made complacent about their suffering.

The distortions caused by sin take many forms and result in much suffering. Moreover, the effects of sin are complex and inescapable; people are both sinners and sinned against. Though appearing in many different forms, sin and its consequences account for most of the reasons why people cannot come to God in faithful worship. Acknowledging this fact is thus an essential starting point for true worship.

Confession of Sin as Orientation to Reality

Because we are sinners, confession is not only a necessary part of worship but also provides a healthy orientation to reality. We have noted above that confessing one's sins does not come naturally. Indeed, to contemporary secular people the idea of "confessing your sins" seems only slightly less offensive than being seen naked in public — they simply see no need to admit their mistakes to anyone, let alone to God. In contemporary Western culture, sin is not a concept that is readily understood. But this blindness to sin is apparently not unique to contemporary culture; biblical writers are aware of this resistance as well. On this point, theologians and biblical witnesses agree: we are not able on our own to recognize our sin for what it is. As Paul says in Romans 3:10-11, quoting Psalm

> And though I behold a man hate me,
> I will love him.
> O God, Father, help me, Father!
> O God, Creator, help me, Father!
> And even though I behold a man hate me,
> I will love him.
>
> From the Dinka of Sudan

14. Justo Gonzáles, *Mañana: Christian Theology from a Hispanic Perspective* (Nashville: Abingdon, 1990), p. 137.

14:1, "There is no one who is righteous, not even one; there is no one who has understanding, there is no one who seeks God." It is only when God illumines our situation, as we stand in the light of God's love manifest in Christ, that we begin to glimpse our own sin. "But now," Paul goes on to say, "apart from law, the righteousness of God has been disclosed . . . through faith in Jesus Christ" (Rom. 3:21-22). And in the light of this righteousness we see ourselves as sinners.

Paul the Apostle provides a good example of this illumination of sin. Before he encountered Christ on the road to Damascus, he considered himself "righteous": he was keeping the law as he understood it, and he was zealous in his religious commitments. But in the light of Christ he came to see all of this as "refuse because of the surpassing value of knowing Christ Jesus my Lord" (Phil. 3:8). In fact, in describing this experience to Agrippa, Paul says that in that encounter God called him to the Gentiles "to open their eyes so that they may turn from darkness to light and from the power of Satan to God, so that they may receive forgiveness of sins" (Acts 26:18).

Thus God by his Spirit must open our eyes to the reality of our sin. This means that just as worship is a response to God's love and call, so confession is a response to his declaration that we are sinners and stand in need of redemption. Though we may feel unable for various reasons to come into worship, it is not these feelings that we express when we confess our sins. Confession of sins responds in the first place to a theological reality — that we are sinners and stand in need of God's deliverance — and not to an emotional one, even if emotions of various kinds may be involved.

Whether we feel it or not, the fact is that apart from grace, we cannot come to God. And neither can we, having come to God in Christ, continue to abide in Christ apart from grace. So the practice of confession in the worship service is a means by which we constantly get reoriented to the way things are. This reorienting is not to the way we think or feel things are, but to the way they actually are. While the world around us may try to convince us that we are really OK, in confession we acknowledge that we constantly go astray, that even our good works are marked by sin, and that apart from God's grace we are lost.

This explains why, in many orders of worship, the confession and pardon come early on, usually just after the call to worship and the opening prayer and hymn. It is a part of what is often called the "gathering" for worship. Other worship liturgies conceive of this basic reorienting process of the confession and pardon in different patterns. The *Lutheran Book of Worship* places the confession and assurance before the opening acts of praise. The *Book of Common Prayer* places it after the proclamation of the Word, as a response to the gospel. Other liturgies place it just before communion.

This theological reorienting is nicely expressed in the classic Anglican prayer of confession. Since we have come together to ask for all those things necessary to salvation, the *Book of Common Prayer* says, "let us kneel in silence, and with penitent and obedient hearts confess our sins, that we may obtain forgiveness by [God's] infinite goodness and mercy." After a time of silence, the prayer of confession is spoken in unison:

> Almighty and most merciful Father, we have erred and strayed from thy ways like lost sheep, we have followed too much the devices and desires of our own hearts, we have offended against thy holy laws, we have left undone those things which we ought to have done, and done those things which we ought not to have done.[15]

Other prayers of confession acknowledge that "our sins are too heavy to carry, too real to hide, and too deep to undo," and "You [God] love us, but we have not loved you/you call, but we have not listened."[16]

An important element of confession, and another aspect of our orientation to reality, is our identification with the larger brokenness of the world. It is here that the working of grace is seen in all its clarity, for, left to ourselves, we would not worry about a broken world. We sometimes do not even recognize the brokenness of the fractured community in which we live. We naturally would worry only about ourselves and our

---

15. *Book of Common Prayer* (New York: Seabury Press, 1979), p. 41.

16. *Book of Common Worship* (Louisville: Westminster/John Knox Press, 1993), pp. 88, 89.

family. But Scripture calls us to a growing identification with and feeling for the divided and fighting world. In the *Book of Common Worship* we are asked to pray, "Although Christ is among us as our peace, we are a people divided against ourselves as we cling to the values of a broken world. The profit and pleasures we pursue lay waste the land and pollute the seas."[17]

We have stressed that confession represents a theological reality rather than an emotional one. But even making this dichotomy risks breaking apart what God intends through worship to bring together. For the object of allowing ourselves to be shaped by these worship practices is that gradually they work on us, until we grow in our feelings, in what older theologians called our godly sorrow, for the brokenness in ourselves and in our world. Here we have much to learn from the African-American tradition of worship, in which deeply felt and often painful memories of the past provide materials for worship. In the "Litany for Holy Communion," the *African American Heritage Hymnal* says, "Let us examine ourselves: our thoughts, our actions, our motives, and our attitudes toward others. O Holy God, have mercy and forgive us our shortcomings." But even more frequently the litanies recall their past:

> Oh God, you have seen the millions of dark bodies buried beneath the tumultuous waves of the deep. Bodies of African men and women who held the seeds of greatness. You have seen women's dream for a united family vanish as they were sold at auction blocks. You have seen the legacy of the African American family decimated and demeaned by those who have attempted to control our destiny. Bitter the chastening rod, felt in the days when hope unborn had died.[18]

Similarly, baptism may be celebrated as that which cleanses from sin, while the people recall that "our ancestors waded in the chilly waters of the South. Through baptism they were made new and free creatures in Christ. 'Jordan River is chilly and cold. It chilled my body, but not my

17. *Book of Common Worship*, p. 88.
18. *African American Heritage Hymnal* (Chicago: GIA Publications, Inc., 2001), p. 74.

soul.'"[19] In a deeply moving way these prayers indicate how the history of these believers has merged with the biblical history. They relive and re-experience this saving history personally and communally.

These prayers remind us of a critical component of the prayers of confession: they are uttered not by individual worshipers but by and on behalf of the community of faith. In fact, Dietrich Bonhoeffer has argued that it is in confession that we break through to community. As he points out, "Sin demands to have a man by himself. It withdraws him from community. . . . But since the confession of sin is made in the presence of the Christian brother, the last stronghold of self-justification is abandoned. . . . Now he stands in the fellowship of sinners who live by the grace of God in the Cross of Jesus Christ."[20] This is the reason that prayer books have frequently incorporated into prayers of confession and repentance the cadences of the Psalter. For the Psalms, though frequently intensely personal, are never private. Indeed, the Psalter was the corporate prayer book of the people of Israel, and now it is also the corporate prayer book of Jewish and Christian believers today.

Those who have suffered deeply are often drawn to the Psalms as they call out to God and utter their corporate cries for help. As the Psalmist says, "Hear my prayer, O LORD; let my cry come to you. Do not hide your face from me in the day of my distress. Incline your ear to me" (Ps. 102:1-2). Sometimes we cannot personally identify with the voice of the Psalmist; it seems too hard or vindictive. So we are tempted to stay with those psalms we can appreciate. But, as Bonhoeffer reminds us, we cannot choose only the comforting psalms, only the psalms of praise. For the psalms of lament are all too real to many suffering Christians today, just as they were real to God's people in Israel. Moreover, they express a suffering that Christ himself has experienced on behalf of his people. Christ joins with the congregation as they confess their sins. As Bonhoeffer puts it,

> A Psalm we cannot utter as a prayer, that makes us falter and horrifies us, is a hint to us that here Someone else is praying, not we; that the

19. *African American Heritage Hymnal*, p. 59.
20. Dietrich Bonhoeffer, *Life Together* (London: SCM, 1954), pp. 87, 88.

One who is here protesting his innocence, who is invoking God's judgment, who has come to such infinite depths of suffering, is none other than Jesus Christ himself. . . . This prayer belongs, not to the individual member, but to the whole body of Christ.[21]

To miss the corporate sense of these prayers is also to miss the way Christ shares in our prayer, just as he shared in the anguish our sin has caused.

The corporate context of confession is underlined in the Christian year when, during Lent, we together remember our frailties and transgressions. The prayers for Ash Wednesday say, "Holy God, we confess to you and to one another, and to the whole communion of saints in heaven and on earth, that we have sinned by our own fault in thought, word, and deed." After the imposition of ashes, "a sign of our mortality and penitence," we say in the litany, "Accomplish in us, O God, the work of your salvation/That we may show forth your glory to the world."[22]

The placement of "confession and pardon" near the beginning of the order of worship, as well as the order of the Christian year, reflects its place at the beginning of our Christian faith. Often Scripture places repentance and faith together to indicate the way that faith is intricately tied to confession. John the Baptist's message of repentance and forgiveness (Mark 1:4) was taken up by Jesus himself (Luke 5:32). Without faith, it is impossible to please God, but without repentance it is impossible to get started in the life of faith. Meanwhile, God patiently waits, as Peter says, "not wanting any to perish, but all to come to repentance" (2 Peter 3:9).

> When there is a gap between me and Christ, when my love is divided, anything can come to fill the gap. Confession is a place where I allow Jesus to take away from me everything that divides, that destroys.
>
> Mother Teresa

21. Bonhoeffer, *Life Together*, pp. 31, 32.
22. *Book of Common Worship*, pp. 225, 227.

Confession and Pardon

We confess our sins in the prayer of confession in gathered worship so that we might hear the good news that we are forgiven in Jesus Christ. The confession of sin is linked theologically to the fact that God has already provided for our sins, once for all, in Jesus Christ. This is why the confession of sin is followed by the pronouncement of forgiveness by the minister. She might say, "Hear the Good News: 'if anyone is in Christ, there is a new creation'" (2 Cor. 5:17), or "If we confess our sins, he who is faithful and just will forgive us our sins and cleanse us from all unrighteousness" (1 John 1:9), or "The LORD is merciful and gracious, slow to anger and abounding in steadfast love. . . . He [the Lord] does not deal with us according to our sins, nor requite us according to our iniquities. For as the heavens are high above the earth, so great is his steadfast love toward those who fear him; as far as the east is from the west, so far does he remove our transgressions from us" (Ps. 103:8, 10-12). And then the words of assurance follow, perhaps in a phrasing like this: "Friends, believe this gospel and go forth to live in peace." The burden of sin is lifted. We can now step out into the peace and reconciliation that Christ has won for us.

In some churches, ministers may use this occasion to pour water into the baptismal font, or dip their hands into the water, to recall the washing of regeneration and the forgiveness represented by baptism. This reminds believers that God has paid for, or covered, the believers' sins in the death of Christ, and by our baptism, through no merit of our own, we have come to share in this cleansing.

Once, when I was a small boy, while throwing snowballs against the wall of our house, I broke a window. I quickly ran in when my mother called me to take a bath — hoping that somehow, in the middle of winter, my parents would not notice what I had done. Later my father came and told me he wanted to show me something. He simply took me outside and pointed to the window that I had broken — now with a new pane of glass in it! I don't remember that he said anything. But in that act, my father made me realize two very important things. First, he quietly made me acknowledge what I had done, something that, on my own, I was reluctant to do. And second, he showed me that someone had gone to the trouble of fixing the window. Someone had paid for my mistake. I often think of this when I come to confession, for few things could have better illustrated to my young mind what is involved in confession and pardon. We must acknowledge what we have done, even though we resist. And yet we must recognize that Someone Else has already paid the price.

But confession and pardon are not an individual reality alone. In thinking about the pardon that God offers us, we must keep in mind the context of the community. Scripture is clear that our forgiveness by God is tied to our willingness to forgive others. As Jesus says in the Sermon on the Mount, "If you forgive others their trespasses, your heavenly Father will also forgive you; but if you do not forgive others, neither will your Father forgive your trespasses" (Matt. 6:14). In the same Gospel, Jesus tells the story of a servant who was deeply in debt and came before his master to plead for his debts to be forgiven. Jesus says, "Out of pity for him, the lord of that slave released him and forgave him the debt" (Matt. 18:27). But that same servant proceeded to go and demand that a fellow slave immediately pay a debt that was owed him. The lord, hearing of this, called the slave to him, asking, "I forgave you all that debt because you pleaded with me. Should you not have had mercy on your fellow slave, as I had mercy on you?" (vv. 32-33). Then the master made the servant pay in full the debt he had owed. Jesus adds, "So my heavenly Father will also do to every one of you, if you do not forgive your brother or sister from your heart!" (v. 35).

Jesus' story and his warning make clear that forgiveness is a corporate reality. It is not a legal transaction only between us and God; forgiveness reorders relationships and thus actually makes things right. The fundamental relationship that needs restoration is, of course, that between us and God. But Scripture does not allow us to separate this relationship from those others that structure our lives, especially those in the body of Christ.

This idea of our responsibility to each other in the community of faith became an important teaching of the Reformers. Luther argued for what he termed the "priesthood of all believers." This means that each person has a direct and unmediated access to God, without the need for the mediation of any human priest. But he also taught that we are called to be priests to one another. Our forgiveness by God places us, in the body of Christ, in the position of mutual responsibility for each other. This means we must confess our sins not only to God but also to each other. Luther explains this in his 1520 treatise *The Babylonian Captivity of the Church*:

> When we have laid bare our conscience to our brother and privately made known to him the evil that lurked within, we receive from our brother's lips the word of comfort spoken by God Himself; and, if we accept it in faith, we find peace in the mercy of God speaking to us through our brother.[23]

This mutual confession is critical, Luther believed, because it makes concrete and real the promises of God. Hearing our brother or sister verbalize for us God's forgiveness further assures us of God's love, even as it makes mutual love real within the body of Christ. Most often it is the pastor who verbalizes for us the words of forgiveness, but there is no reason why we should not cultivate the practice, as members of the congregation, of assuring each other that God has forgiven us through Christ. John Wesley meant this to be an integral part of the way Christians support each other week by week; this practice could perhaps be incorporated into the ministry of small groups.

But forgiveness is very difficult. Indeed, it is nothing short of a divine gift. It is precisely the difficulty of mutual forgiveness that makes necessary the repeated practice of confession in the service of worship. Confessing our own sins week by week, again and again, reminds us of our own dependence on the boundless grace of God.

The sheer generosity of God's grace was a difficult concept for Jesus' disciples to understand. Peter once asked Jesus, "Lord, if another member of the church sins against me, how often should I forgive? As many as seven times?" (Matt. 18:21). Peter had come to understand from Jesus'

---

23. *A Compendium of Luther's Theology*, ed. Hugh T. Kerr (Philadelphia: Westminster Press, 1963), p. 97.

teaching that we need to be a forgiving community, but of course this has limits, he thought. Seven times seemed to him to be sufficient; beyond that, surely, a fellow believer is abusing this grace. "Not seven times," Jesus answered, "but, I tell you, seventy times seven" (v. 22). This appears to be a Jewish expression for a limitless number. The bottom line is that we are never to stop forgiving. Because God has forgiven our sins (Isa. 43:25), we should forgive the sins of others. In this respect, we are to imitate God.

Passing the Peace of Christ

In many services, after the pronouncement of pardon by the minister, the people are invited to share the peace of Christ. Having been reconciled to God in Jesus Christ, the people are asked to share the unity and love that comes only from God. In the *Book of Common Worship*, the minister says, "Since God has forgiven us in Christ, let us forgive one another. The peace of our Lord Jesus Christ be with you all."[24] The people respond, in unison, "And also with you." They then turn to each other and say, "Peace be with you." In some congregations, this is a missed opportunity. People instead say, "Good morning." The missed opportunity is this: When we look at one another and say, "The peace of the Lord Jesus Christ be with you," we are extending to one another the reality that, having been reconciled to God, we are also reconciled to one another. The act suggests that we do more than simply forget their slights and trespasses against us; we actually reach out to them in love and communion. I am often struck by the fact that, though I often do not feel like greeting people, the very act of doing so reminds me of my relationship to them and of our mutual responsibilities. And carrying out this act frequently brings with it feelings of love and unity. Here we model God's action in which God reaches out and embraces us in Christ and calls us to the ministry of reconciliation. We embrace each other on behalf of God.

24. *Book of Common Worship*, p. 57.

Foot Washing

In some churches the practice of washing one another's feet is practiced as an ordinance or sacrament of humility and mutual responsibility. In some it is particularly associated with the Maundy Thursday service. The practice derives from Jesus' washing the disciples' feet in John 13. John locates this event very precisely: before the Passover, when Jesus knew that his "hour to depart" had come and when the devil had put it into the heart of Judas to betray Jesus (vv. 1-3). At this point, John says, Jesus "got up from the table, took off his outer robe, and tied a towel around himself. Then he poured water into a basin and began to wash the disciples' feet" (vv. 4-5). In his commentary, Raymond Brown says that the Gospel of John is like a great pendulum swinging down from heaven and reaching back to heaven.[25] At precisely this point in chapter 13, Jesus has reached the lowest point of his self-emptying service. Here, he voluntarily takes a towel to wash the disciples' feet.

In New Testament times, the act of washing someone's feet was considered servile, the work of a slave, or perhaps of a woman or child in that patriarchal culture. In John's account, Peter objects to having Jesus wash his feet, and Jesus answers, "Unless I wash you, you have no share with me" (v. 8). Lest the disciples miss the lesson he is giving them, a few verses later Jesus says, "If I, your Lord and Teacher, have washed your feet, you also ought to wash one another's feet" (v. 14). Though attested elsewhere in the New Testament (1 Tim. 5:10), foot washing seems not to have been formally practiced in the early church before the seventh century.[26] In America it has been associated with the Church of the Brethren, though it is more widely practiced in the Maundy Thursday service.

A foot-washing liturgy is usually begun with the reading of John 13. Typically water is poured into a basin, and a group of people come

25. Raymond Brown, *The Gospel According to John* (Garden City, N.Y.: Doubleday, 1970), pp. 541, 542.

26. See "Pedilavium," *Oxford Dictionary of the Christian Church*, 2d ed. (Oxford: Oxford University Press, 1974), and "Footwashing," *Dictionary of Christianity in America* (Downers Grove, Ill.: InterVarsity Press, 1990).

forward and have their feet washed, then change places with those washing their feet. It is a tactile and expressive sign both of humility and of the mutual obligation believers have to one
another — both of which
recall the action of Jesus
for his disciples. It is an
enacted parable of this in-
junction of Paul: "Look
not to your own interests,
but to the interests of others. Let the same mind be
in you that was in Christ
Jesus, who, though he was
in the form of God, did
not regard equality with
God as something to be
exploited, but emptied
himself, taking the form
of a slave" (Phil. 2:4-7).

> Without forgiveness, the social power of a closed circle may crush its members, soil itself, and sour its social world. Examples of such soured communitarianism litter the pages of every honest church history. But with forgiveness controlling everything, the closed circle is opened, the forgiven forgivers' practice of community is redeemed and becomes positively redemptive; thus this powerful practice renders obedience to the law of the Lord Jesus Christ.
>
> James William McClendon

Confession and the Larger Celebration of Redemption

The confession of sin and the assurance of pardon express the heart and reality of the gospel. The announcement by the minister — "Hear the good news: in Jesus Christ, you are forgiven" — reminds us that this moment of the liturgy, humble though it may seem, actually points us to the center of our worship. It reorients us to our true identity; it reorders our relationships; it gives us a taste of the shalom that will someday be ours in abundance. The forgiveness we receive from God makes everything else possible, both in worship and in our life before God. It is the pearl of great price for which we are called to sell everything. And, having sold everything, this practice reminds us, we are given back in Christ everything pertaining to life and godliness.

The moments of confession and pardon recall Alyosha's experience of conversion in Dostoevsky's *The Brothers Karamazov*. Alyosha, "overflowing with rapture," throws himself down on the earth, embracing himself and kissing everything. Looking at the earth and at the stars, he realizes, "There seemed to be threads from all those innumerable worlds of God, linking his soul to them, and it was trembling all over 'in contact with other worlds.' He longed to forgive everyone and for everything and to beg forgiveness. Oh, not for himself, but for all men, for all and for everything."[27]

It is as though in the simple practice of confession and assurance, which takes but a minute or two in the service, we are led through the entire story of redemption; we are called, as Luther liked to say, to "remember our baptism" in our going down into the waters and our rising again. As in Dante's great pilgrimage, this practice speaks of our great voyage in God, our descent down into hell itself and then our journey up through purgatory to paradise. We confess; we are forgiven. This speaks of the story of God's people, who go down into Egypt and are brought back through the waters into the promised land. It recalls the dispersion into exile, and God's descent all the way down into the brokenness of creation in Christ. And it recalls Jesus, who, when he realizes that the end has come, takes a towel and becomes a servant even to the point of death. But it celebrates the fact that after his descent into hell, Christ comes up out of the grave and ascends to the Father, where he prepares for the celebration of the marriage supper of the Lamb (Rev. 19:9).

The confession of sin and the assurance of pardon in the worship service enact the great movements of descending and rising in the Christian faith. The theological enormity of these moments is daunting. But the fresh honesty and grace of these moments are so full of release and hope that, as Anne Lamott said in a flash of insight, every week in gathered worship, we are, by the gracious love of God, "tricked into coming back to life."

---

27. Fyodor Dostoevsky, *The Brothers Karamazov*, ed. Edmund Fuller (New York: Dell, 1956), p. 253. Alyosha also realizes that "others are praying for me too."

We Cannot Measure How You Heal

We cannot measure how you heal
or answer every sufferer's prayer,
yet we believe your grace responds
where faith and doubt unite to care.
Your hands, though bloodied on the cross,
survive to hold and heal and warn,
to carry all through death to life
and cradle children yet unborn.

The pain that will not go away,
the guilt that clings from things long past,
the fear of what the future holds,
are present as if meant to last.
But present too is love which tends
the hurt we never hoped to find,
the private agonies inside,
the memories that haunt the mind.

So some have come who need your help,
and some have come to make amends,
as hands which shaped and saved the world
are present in the touch of friends.
Lord, let your Spirit meet us here
to mend the body, mind and soul,
to disentangle peace from pain
and make your broken people whole.

John L. Bell (b. 1949)

Children from Your Vast Creation

Children from your vast creation
gather here for guidance, Lord;
we of every tongue and nation
yearn to see your earth restored.
You have shown that your intention
wills a world kept free from strife.
Open us to love's dimension,
filled with true abundant life.

We have grasped for more possessions,
wanting things we do not need;
help us, Lord, lest our obsessions
soon consume us in our greed.
Cure our tendency to plunder —
scarring forests, wasting ore.
Come and turn our schemes asunder;
take away our lust for more.

We are learning how much damage
spreads throughout the world from greed;
though you made us in your image,
we are less than you decreed.
Wanting ease and pleasure strongly,
craving things your love deplores,
asking not, or asking wrongly,
we resort to waging wars.

Lord, we come as sisters, brothers,
seeking your redemptive touch.
Let unselfish love for others triumph,
lest we want too much.
Come to us amid life's scrimmage;
help your people live as one.
Recreate us in your image;
speed the day your will is done!

David A. Robb (b. 1932)

Proclamation | Revelation, Christology

Leanne Van Dyk

Rembrandt, the famous seventeenth-century Dutch artist, painted several depictions of the story of the Emmaus disciples in the Gospel of Luke. One of the paintings portrays the exact moment when Jesus is recognized over the breaking of bread at the evening meal. One disciple reacts with surprise. His hands are thrown back, his eyes round, his mouth ready — any second — to exclaim, "Oh, it's Jesus!" The light of the candle spotlights the disciple's face at that incredible moment.

The other disciple is oblivious. He is in the shadows. He shows no recognition. No surprise. He simply isn't paying attention at all! Rembrandt puts another character in the story as well, one that Luke doesn't mention in the Gospel text. He is a servant in the background, hardly visible in the shadows, bending over a sink, washing up the supper dishes. The servant, too, is oblivious to the real identity of Jesus Christ. For him, this dinner is no different than any other, this guest no different than any other.

This painting can serve as a metaphor for the experience of worship week after week for many Christian believers. For some, the worship service is a revelation: they see and know and experience God in worship. God is there! For others, the worship service reveals nothing. God is absent. God remains obscure, unrecognized.

Yet, Christians gather each Sunday to worship God in the name of Jesus Christ. They gather in response to God's call. They pray for the illumination of the Holy Spirit before the reading of Scripture and the hearing of the sermon. They receive the bread and cup of the Lord's Supper. They pray. They sing. They give their offerings. They receive the benediction. They go out to serve in faith and love. For some believers, the worship service is a consistent time of nourishment and joy. Other believers go in the door hopefully but leave discouraged. For them, the service feels dreary, joyless. Why, they wonder, does a faith with such *good news* produce worship that displays so little of it? Still other believers sink the anchor of their faith into one particular part of the worship service — the sermon or the Scripture or the hymns. In Wendell Berry's novel *Jayber Crow*, the young bachelor Jayber gives a brief account of what sustains his own spiritual life:

> What I liked least about the service itself was the prayers; what I liked far better was the singing. Not all of the hymns could move me. I never liked "Onward, Christian Soldiers" or "The Battle Hymn of the Republic." Jesus' military career has never compelled my belief. I liked the sound of the people singing together, whatever they sang, but some of the hymns reached into me all the way to the bone: "Come, Thou Fount of Every Blessing," "Rock of Ages," "Amazing Grace," "O God, Our Help in Ages Past." I loved the different voices all singing one song, the various tongues and qualities, the passing lifts of feeling, rising up and going out forever. Old Man Profet, who was a different man on Sunday, used to draw out the notes at the ends of verses and refrains so he could listen to himself, and in fact it sounded pretty. And when the congregation would be singing, "We shall see the King some day (some-day)," Sam May, who often protracted Saturday night a little too far into Sunday morning, would sing, "*I* shall see the King some-day (Sam May)." . . . And in times of sorrow when they sang "Abide with Me," I could not raise my head.[1]

For any Christian believer who wonders if God is really present in worship, the Christian tradition has a confident and vigorous Trinitarian reply. Christian worship is fundamentally our participation, through the Holy Spirit, in Jesus Christ's communion with God the Fa-

1. Wendell Berry, *Jayber Crow* (New York: Counterpoint Press, 2000), pp. 162-63.

ther.[2] Not only is God present with us in worship; we are present with God within God's own Trinitarian life. The Trinitarian character of a worship service is seen from beginning to end.[3] God's presence is proclaimed at the beginning of the service in the call to worship. The presence of Jesus Christ is visible in the sacramental signs of water, bread, and wine. The Holy Spirit is invoked in the prayer of illumination before the reading of Scripture and in the epiclesis before the words of institution in the Lord's Supper.

> [The Word of God] took pity on our race, and had mercy on our infirmity, and condescended to our corruption, and, unable to bear that death should have the mastery — lest the creature should perish, and his Father's handiwork in [us] be spent for nought — he takes unto himself a body, and that of no different sort from ours.
>
> Athanasius

Yet the presence of the triune God is also unavoidably veiled and hidden. When Moses asked God to reveal to him the full measure of divine glory, God replied that Moses could not see God's glory and live.[4] True, Scripture sometimes reports satisfying, full-scale divine theophanies, like the fire from heaven that consumed the water-drenched altar on Mount Carmel, with the priests of Baal looking on in horrified amazement. More often, however, God chooses to work on the human scale, in the ordinary ebb and flow of life. Worship is a miracle of grace; it is God who calls us to gather together to reorient our frayed and tattered selves each week. But it is also a gathering of human beings who peer at one another and at God, hoping and waiting for a glimpse of glory.

A friend of mine who is a pastor once said something particularly

2. James Torrance develops this Trinitarian understanding of Christian worship in his book *Worship, Community, and the Triune God of Grace* (Downers Grove, Ill.: InterVarsity Press, 1996).

3. See the opening chapter for a fuller description of the Trinitarian character of worship.

4. Cf. Exodus 33:17-23.

memorable to me when I was expressing my frustration about worship that is often tedious rather than transcendent. "God sometimes chooses to be present in odd, offbeat ways to a particular person," he explained. "It's not always in the sermon, or the prayers, or the hymns. Sometimes it's just in a moment — a line of a text in the hymn, the passing of the peace, the singing of the doxology — *something.*" Then his voice caught, his eyes filled with tears, and he said, "God came to earth in a messy, ordinary birth. Sometimes God will reach out in something totally ordinary, something messy even, in the worship service — a sullen kid, an old, lingering argument between two elders — it can be anything, anything *human* — because that's the way God comes to us: God comes to us in *human* form. That's called the Incarnation. The thing is, you have to be alert to how God is going to speak to you, because if you're not alert, if you're not ready, you'll miss it. You have to go to church expectant, ready to catch what God is going to say."

That was one of the best sermons I ever heard. It was a reminder that God chooses the lowly things of this world — the words of a preacher, the text and tune of a hymn — and God uses them to reveal God's own divine self, to impart God's grace, mercy, and love, and to unite believers with one another and with God.

This chapter will explore the multiple connections between what Christians confess, namely, the love of God in Jesus Christ our Lord, and what Christians do, namely, worship God in liturgy and in life. Specifically, this chapter will explore the connections between the *Word of God,* Jesus Christ, and the *word of God,* usually understood to be the Scripture and the sermon, although we will see that the meanings that ripple out from the phrase *word of God* are richer than what we are often accustomed to consider.

There is, of course, a familiar ambiguity to the term "Word of God." What precisely does it mean? It is exactly right for a Christian believer to say, "Well, it depends on how you're using that phrase. Jesus Christ is *the* Word of God. But the Bible is the word of God, too. The sermon, also, is the word of God. The Lord's Supper is a visible word of God. And God's word comes in other ways as well." Such a believer would thoughtfully be reflecting on the wide variety of ways we understand the phrase.

Karl Barth (1886-1968) organized the discussion by suggesting that there are three forms of the Word of God.[5] The Word of God, first and foremost, is Jesus Christ. Second, the word of God is Scripture, as it witnesses to Jesus Christ. Third, the word of God is preaching as it finds its source in Scripture. Barth's purpose in formulating the threefold form of the Word of God was to make clear the relationship between Jesus Christ, Scripture, and the sermon.

The Word of God: Jesus Christ

The Word of God, first and foremost, is Jesus Christ. Jesus Christ is the Word of God *par excellence*. "In the beginning was the Word, and the Word was with God, and the Word was God," the prologue to John's Gospel begins. The opening verses of this gospel give the briefest outline of a *logos* (or Word) Christology. Reaching deep into both Greek and Jewish traditions, the author of the Gospel conveyed a complex set of ideas: that the Word was not only in the beginning with God but was also the principle by which all things came into being and the very foundation of reality. The rich ideas of *logos* Christology can be seen elsewhere in the New Testament as well, such as Colossians 1:15 — "He is the image of the invisible God, the firstborn of all creation" — and Hebrews 1:3: "He is the reflection of God's glory and the exact imprint of God's very being, and he sustains all things by his powerful word."

This Word, the very life force of all that is, came to earth for us and our salvation. The Word of God was born as Jesus of Nazareth, son of Mary and Joseph. He was born in an ad hoc homeless shelter to a young unwed mother. These very particular circumstances of the birth of Jesus Christ are sometimes called the "scandal of particularity." The particularity of the Incarnation — *this* child, *this* time, *this* place — is both the

---

5. This has not been an uncontroversial suggestion. Some theologians, most notably the American theologian Cornelius Van Til (1895-1987), have seen Barth's threefold form of the Word of God as problematic and have vigorously criticized it as potentially undermining the authority and inspiration of Scripture.

scandal and the comfort of the Christian faith. Self-sufficient modern people resist the centrality and necessity of God's revelation in Christ; on good days, we really believe we can handle things ourselves. This is the scandal. Lonely, isolated modern people, on bad days, desperately need the affirmation and acceptance of their human limitations in the Incarnation. This is the comfort. Immanuel, "God-with-us," also means "God-with-me" and "God-with-you."

God spoke God's Word into human flesh in the Incarnation in the birth of Jesus of Nazareth. Jesus Christ, in his life of teachings and healings, in his relationships with women, children, and outcasts, continued not only to speak but also to embody God's word to those who would listen and see. But it was in the climactic final days of his life that Jesus' identity as the Word of God became more vivid. In fact, the biblical writers, in their effort to grasp the full meaning of those final days of Jesus' trial, execution, and resurrection, would require a much wider range of metaphors, including Lamb of God, Son of God, Final Sacrifice, Victor, Great High Priest, Son of Man, and King of the Ages. The "Word of God" is a key biblical image referring to Jesus Christ, but it is not the only important image. Biblical writers, theologians, mystics, devotional writers, hymn-text writers, and believers who pray every day search for the right words to express the truth of God's saving love to us in Jesus Christ.

The great fourth-century theologian Athanasius described the plight of confused, lost, and sinful human beings in his treatise *On the Incarnation of the Word*. Once human beings had stumbled from the path of obedience and faithfulness that God had originally laid out for them, they were utterly incapable of finding the way back again. They were helpless, hopeless, hapless creatures of the dark. Athanasius skillfully illuminates not only the plight of lost humanity but also, in a very real sense, the plight of God. He asks again and again, "What was God to do?" After all, God had said that if humans foolishly disobeyed God's commands, they would die. God's truthfulness could not fail to exact the penalty so clearly stipulated. Yet, God's goodness and mercy yearned for the restoration of the fallen creation. So then, what was God to do, asked Athanasius. How was it possible for God "to keep still silence at so great a thing, and suffer men to be led astray by demons and not to know God?"[6]

The good news of the Christian faith is that God did not "keep still silence." God spoke. God spoke through prophets and through God's law to God's covenant people. And God's people spoke right back, in worship and praise and prayer. Then, in God's good time, God uttered a Word that pierced the silence of our ignorance and confusion, a Word that became flesh and lived among us, full of grace and truth.

There are a number of key images for Jesus in the New Testament. "In the beginning was the Word." Jesus is the Word. "The light shines in the darkness, and the darkness did not overcome it." Jesus is also the Light. We, who were ignorant, now hear. We, who were in darkness, now see.

Jesus as Word and Light, both images introduced in the first chapter of John's Gospel, are important for our consideration of the worship service. Jesus Christ is God's Word to a world deaf to the truth. Jesus Christ is God's Light to a world blind to the truth. In worship, we hear that truth and see that light. Jesus Christ is truly present with us. But how?

There are a variety of ways to answer that question. When I was a child, I would have simply said, "Jesus Christ is present in my heart." In Sunday School we used to sing a song with a simple text and a galloping rhythm that shaped my budding theological imagination. I still remember the chorus text:

He lives, he lives, Christ Jesus lives today!
He walks with me and talks with me along life's narrow way.
He lives, he lives, salvation to impart!
You ask me how I know he lives? He lives within my heart.

Perhaps Sunday School curricula do not include this old hymn any longer. But one of the first theological concepts of very young children is that Jesus lives in their hearts. Jesus is present *in* them. There is nothing

6. Athanasius, *On the Incarnation of the Word*, in *Christology of the Later Fathers*, ed. E. Hardy and C. Richardson (Philadelphia: Westminster Press, 1954), p. 67.

wrong with that childlike answer to the question of Jesus' presence with us. But just as the Apostle Paul recognized that his understanding of the faith needed to "grow up" as he matured in the faith (1 Cor. 13:11), so our understanding of Jesus' presence with us deepens as well.

Christ is truly present with us by the power of the Holy Spirit, who unites us to himself in the reading of Scripture, in the preaching of the sermon, in the forgiveness of sins, in acts of service and compassion, in the celebration of the sacrament, and in the entire worship service. The Holy Spirit unites us to each other in the community of faith and unites us to Jesus Christ. "We are one in the Spirit, we are one in the Lord," says the familiar praise chorus. This "oneness" we share in community is a gift of the Spirit, who unites us to Christ and, in so doing, makes Christ present in us and to us.

> The narratives of scripture were not meant to describe our world . . . but to change the world, including the one in which we now live.
>
> Stanley Hauerwas

First Corinthians 12, in which Paul describes the church as the body of Christ, is the classic biblical text that illustrates this insight. If the church, with all its individual members, all its differently gifted people, is the body of Christ, then Jesus Christ is present in the church as it lives out its life together. No better place does this communal heart beat than in the worship service, and then in the life that flows out from the worship service into the world.

Because Jesus Christ is truly present with us in the reading of Scripture, in the preaching of the sermon, in the celebration of the sacrament, and throughout the worship service, in these moments we are brought into the very life of the triune God. This is an astonishing thought, one for which, echoing a remark of Annie Dillard, we should all wear crash helmets.[7] In worship, we participate in Christ's communion with the Father by the power of the Holy Spirit. This is what true worship is: our participation in inner-Trinitarian communion. Not only is Jesus Christ

---

7. Annie Dillard, *Teaching a Stone to Talk* (New York: HarperCollins, 1982), p. 52.

present with us, but we are present to the triune God and brought into the divine life. This resonant answer to the question "How is Jesus Christ present to us in worship?" reaches back to the patristic voices in the Christian tradition. It is characteristic of Calvin as well, in his language of "union with Christ" and his rich sacramental theology.

James Torrance sees a continuity of this patristic theological idea with the central theme of the book of Hebrews. He identifies that theme in this way: "Jesus Christ is the leader of our worship, the high priest who forgives us our sins and leads us into the holy presence of the Father."[8] Hebrews sets up a contrast between the "first covenant" (9:1), which was expressed in an earthly sanctuary, and the new, fulfilled covenant, with Christ as the mediator. Indeed, "Christ did not enter a sanctuary made by human hands, a mere copy of the true one, but he entered into heaven itself, now to appear in the presence of God on our behalf" (9:24). Perhaps the theme of Hebrews is summed up most succinctly in the wonderful summary of faith in chapter 4:

> Since, then, we have a great high priest who has passed through the heavens, Jesus, the Son of God, let us hold fast to our confession. For we do not have a high priest who is unable to sympathize with our weaknesses, but we have one who in every respect has been tested as we are, yet without sin. Let us therefore approach the throne of grace with boldness, so that we may receive mercy and find grace to help in time of need. (vv. 14-16)

Jesus Christ is present in our worship because Jesus Christ is the leader of our worship. It is he who, sympathizing with our weaknesses, ushers us to the throne of grace through the power of the Holy Spirit. It is foolish for us to imagine that we can casually stroll into the presence of God. "O LORD, who may abide in your tent? Who may dwell on your holy hill?" asks Psalm 15. The answer, in the next line of the psalm, would seem to exclude every one of us: "Those who walk blamelessly, and do what is right." We don't deserve to worship God. But God graciously invites us to worship and then provides us with the means to receive com-

---

8. Torrance, *Worship, Community, and the Triune God of Grace*, p. 57.

munion with and revelation from God — the very presence of Christ, by the power of the Holy Spirit. This is Trinitarian mystery, hospitality, and gift.

The Word of God: Scripture

"Let the word of God dwell in you richly," says the Apostle Paul to the church in Colossae (3:16). This text does not specifically refer to Scripture. In fact, Paul knew nothing of the New Testament as we know it. The Gospels were most likely still in oral form when he penned his letters to the young churches in Asia Minor; these letters were circulating as documents of instruction and encouragement. The New Testament as authoritative Scripture was still a distant reality. But it may be that Paul was referring to the Bible that he *did* know — the Hebrew Bible. And this verse certainly can be understood by Christians today to refer to both Old and New Testaments. "Let the word of God dwell in you richly." It is interesting to notice that the rest of the verse places Scripture as the word of God solidly in the context of the worship service: "Teach and admonish one another in all wisdom; and with gratitude in your hearts sing psalms, hymns, and spiritual songs to God."

How it is, exactly, that Scripture is the word of God is not immediately obvious or clear. How can *these* ancient words from *those* ancient cultures be God's word to us today? This is a scandal of particularity analogous to the scandal of particularity of the Incarnation. Especially in the past two or three hundred years, since the tides of Enlightenment rationalism and evidentialism have washed up on the intellectual shores of the church's consciousness, Christians have struggled with *how* the Bible is the word of God. The question that immediately follows, for our inquiry in this chapter, is how the Bible is the word of God in the worship service: How is Jesus Christ present to us in worship through Scripture?

Theologian John Burgess helps us consider this question by reviewing various understandings of the Bible in his book *Why Scripture Matters*. First, there is the "propositional" understanding of the Bible. On this view, the Bible sets forth revealed truths about God. These truths might be theological, such as "God so loved the world that God's Son came into the world to save sinners." Or these truths might be ethical, such as "Envying what your neighbor has is wrong." In any case, the truths contained in the Bible can be stated in propositions. This is what it means that the Bible is the word of God. Burgess calls this position the "orthodox" position.[9]

Another common understanding of the Bible as the word of God might be called the symbolic position, or what Burgess calls the "progressivist" position.[10] On this view, the Bible is a repository of symbols and stories that express the religious longings of the human spirit and help us interpret our own religious longings. The Bible is the word of God, then, in the sense that it helps us find the word of God in our own experience; it *points* to the word of God that we discover in our own lives; it may offer analogies, metaphors, and markers to show how God is speaking to us now.

The "orthodox" and "progressivist" understandings of Scripture, however, are not the only and (fortunately) not the most helpful in grasping the character of Scripture as the word of God as it functions in worship. Burgess suggests another way. Scripture is the word of God in the sense that it is a *sacramental word*. Scripture presents Christ to the believing community. "As a sacramental word," Burgess says, "Scripture is not only a witness, however unique or authoritative, to the revelation that has taken place in Christ; rather, Scripture as *Scripture* also sets forth the living Christ. It draws us into Christ's presence and invites us to be

---

9. John Burgess, *Why Scripture Matters: Reading the Bible in a Time of Church Conflict* (Louisville: Westminster/John Knox Press, 1998), p. 41. For a fuller typology of views of Scripture, see the more complex typology of Avery Dulles in *Models of Revelation* (Garden City, N.Y.: Image Books, 1985). There are some interesting and complex overlaps between issues of the nature of Scripture as the word of God and the nature of the inspiration of Scripture. This latter issue will not be dealt with in this chapter.

10. The terms "orthodox" and "progressivist" are not altogether helpful terms, as Burgess himself indicates by enclosing these terms in quotation marks whenever he refers to them. They strain under caricature and crack under pejorative usage. Here they are intended only as a rough, descriptive typology.

transformed into his image. It opens the possibility of relationship between the divine and the human."[11]

On this view, Scripture *forms* the community into the body of
Christ. This happens most centrally in the worship service. Although
certainly it can and does happen in private devotion and prayer, it happens paradigmatically in communal worship. Burgess says, "When Scripture is read, when it is explicated in preaching, when it is incorporated
into prayers of thanksgiving and lament, when it frames the celebration
of the Lord's Supper, Scripture be-comes a means by which Christians
are gathered into the body of the living Lord."[12] Scripture is a "means of
grace" used by the Holy Spirit to nourish and build up the community
of faith. The Spirit uses the words of the text in much the same way that
the Spirit uses the water of baptism and the bread and wine of the Lord's
Supper to form the community of faith and to unite believers to Jesus
Christ. The Holy Spirit uses Scripture as a sacramental "element," as it
were, to unite the believer to Christ.

> Preaching is finally more than art or science. It is al-chemy, in which tin be-comes gold and yard rocks become diamonds under the influence of the Holy Spirit. It is a process of transformation for both the preacher and congregation alike, as the ordinary de-tails of their everyday lives are translated into the ex-traordinary elements of God's ongoing creation.
>
> Barbara Brown Taylor

No claim is being made here that the Bible is a "third sacrament."[13]
Rather, this is a perspective on one particularly fruitful way of understanding how Scripture is the word of God: Scripture is the word of God
in that, through faith and by the Spirit, Scripture unites believers to Jesus
Christ, himself the Word of God. The Bible is the word of God in a sacra-

---

11. Burgess, *Why Scripture Matters*, p. 43.
12. Burgess, *Why Scripture Matters*, p. 43.
13. Or, in the case of the Roman Catholic tradition, an eighth sacrament!

mental sense, uniting us to Christ, the one true Word of God. Just as the Lord's Supper, through the power of the Holy Spirit, brings Christ and the believing community together in a feast of thanksgiving and communion, so Scripture, through the power of the Holy Spirit, brings Christ to believers. Theologian David Yeago explains, "Scripture functions as a quasi-sacramental instrument of the Holy Spirit, through which the Spirit makes known the mystery of Christ in order to form the church as a sign of his messianic dominion."[14] This is most richly and dramatically understood in the context of communal worship, when the people of God are gathered together, united as the body of Christ.

But Scripture does not just remain in the pew racks in the worship service. It is read. It is read aloud. Here we make a rather startling claim: when Scripture is read in gathered worship, *Christ is presented* to the community of believers. This rather simple affirmation has profound implications for the worship service. At the very least, it implies that the reading of Scripture ought to be done with preparation and care. Haphazard or careless reading of the Scripture text is inappropriate. Reading in a false and pretentious voice is unfitting. A clear and well-delivered reading presents no barriers to either the people's hearing or the work of the Holy Spirit.

Yet this goal does not mean that only the ordained minister ought to read the Scripture text in the worship service. The well-read word can include the multigenerational spectrum of the life of the congregation. Readers' workshops can, for example, be a feature of the church's life together, a regularly scheduled event where children, youth, and adults can work together, rehearsing the Sunday texts and receiving coaching from an experienced reader. Excellent Scripture reading can be planned, modeled, and valued in a congregation.[15]

The reading of the Scripture text is dramatic divine revelation. "We

14. David S. Yeago, "The Bible," in *Knowing the Triune God: The Work of the Spirit in the Practices of the Church* (Grand Rapids: Eerdmans, 2001), p. 50.

15. This is one small example of the integration of worship and theology: a congregation's theology of the Word is expressed in the care it takes with the reading of the Scripture texts. Likewise, the patterns of a congregation's habits of preparation for reading the Scripture texts reveal their theology of the Word.

might sum up the event of the reading of the Word by saying that then the Word which had been in chains, imprisoned by the letters of the alphabet, comes alive," says the Swiss Reformed theologian J. J. von Allmen.[16] He even claims that the gospel is "enclosed in the letter of the Bible and must be freed." The venerable tradition of Bible study and meditation is by no means dismissed in this statement. It simply highlights the importance of the public reading of Scripture in the worship service. Von Allmen then gives a rather stern rebuke to "the protestant mania for remarks before or after each reading," advising pastors and lay readers to "follow the rule of simplicity" in a clear and dignified reading of the text.[17]

The "frame" of the reading of the biblical text can assist worshipers to await God's revelation expectantly and eagerly. To signal a deep hunger and thirst for the word of God before the reading of the text, the reader might say, "Listen to these words from the book that we love." Or the traditional acclamations can be used. "Glory to you, O Lord!" before and "Praise to you, O Christ!" following the Scripture reading establish a context in which the spoken text can become the particular, "incarnate" word of God. These traditional liturgical formulae declare to the people that, as David Yeago puts it, "these are the deeds and utterances of one who is living and at large, not dead and confined to the tomb, one who is present and able to act, who has indeed been enthroned as Lord and Christ."[18]

"Worship is Scripture's home," says Aiden J. Kavanagh, a liturgical theologian. He means, at the very least, that "the liturgy must be awash in Scripture."[19] The words of Scripture are not to be confined only to

16. J. J. von Allmen, *Worship: Its Theology and Practice* (Oxford: Oxford University Press, 1968), p. 132. This might be a good place to signal the vexing issue of the correct use of the uppercase and lowercase "w" in "word of God." All authors use the uppercase with respect to Christ. Consistency breaks down with respect to Scripture and preaching. Some authors use the uppercase with respect to Scripture and preaching; others use the lowercase. Context is the clue.

17. Von Allmen, *Worship*, p. 137.

18. Yeago, "The Bible," p. 55.

19. Aidan J. Kavanagh, "Scriptural Word and Liturgical Worship," in *Reclaiming the Bible for the Church*, ed. C. Braaten and R. Jensen (Grand Rapids: Eerdmans, 1995), p. 136.

their reading before the sermon. The worship service must properly be soaked in Scripture. The pastor or liturgists can speak Scripture; their hearts, minds, and imaginations must be so filled with Scripture that the worship service itself will be filled with the words of Scripture.[20] If done well — naturally and genuinely — this will not be false or stiff. No one will think to say, "Just say it in your own words," because they will see that these words of Scripture *are* the words that come straight from the heart. The magnificent hymn "I Bind unto Myself Today" begins with the familiar line "I bind unto myself today the strong name of the Trinity," but it includes a lesser-known line: "I bind unto myself today the Word of God to give me speech." Without binding ourselves both to Jesus Christ and to Scripture, we are as good as mute.

Throughout the worship service, on this model, Scripture could be used. The service might begin with the sturdy sentences of Psalm 46: "God is our refuge and strength, a very present help in trouble." Psalm 51, which begins "Have mercy on me, O God, according to your steadfast love; according to your abundant mercy, blot out my transgressions," is a prayer of confession that strikes at the heart of every sinner in need of God's gracious pardon. The psalms of lament give voice to a congregation in times of grief or sorrow. Lament psalms must not be overlooked for what, in some congregational cultures, is the official language of cheer and optimism.[21] The service might end with one of the lovely Pauline benedictions or the stately Aaronic benediction: "The LORD bless you and keep you; the LORD make his face to shine upon you, and be gracious to you; the LORD lift up his countenance upon you, and give you peace."

A worship service in which all words spoken, from first to last, are words *from Scripture* — such a service will be rigged and ready to sail into the waters that flow from the throne room of God (Rev. 22). God has chosen, in mysterious divine wisdom, this collection of documents that

20. I owe this insight to Timothy Brown.

21. Daniel Migliore and Kathleen Billman note that the psalms of lament are underrepresented in liturgies of several mainline denominational resources. Cf. *Rachel's Cry: Prayer of Lament and Rebirth of Hope* (Cleveland: United Church Press, 1999), p. 13.

comprise our Bible to be the means by which we are formed to be the people of faith. God has chosen, in mysterious divine wisdom, this Bible to be one of the means by which Christ is presented to us in our gathered worship. God has chosen, in mysterious divine wisdom, this Bible to be the means of our comfort, judgment, instruction, hope, lament, and vision. It would be a great folly for us to fill our worship service with words — mountains of words — that do not find their source in this God-appointed well.

The Word of God: Preaching

The Second Helvetic Confession, a sixteenth-century confession of faith written by the Zürich Protestant Reformer Heinrich Bullinger, famously states that "the preaching of the Word of God is the Word of God." Preachers who are even marginally self-aware know keenly the paradox of the comfort and the scandal of the sermon. The comfort of knowing that the sermon can and does become the word of God for the people is what gives the preacher, despite fears and failings, the courage to face the congregation each Sunday morning. The scandal that the word of God is housed in the poor words of the preacher and then set free by the Spirit is a stumbling block as well — a stumbling block to the preacher, who may feel discouraged; to the believer, who may sense the poverty of the sermon; and perhaps even to the nonbeliever, who does not, or does not yet, hear the good news of the gospel.

Novels and movies frequently portray preachers as hucksters, entertainers, or incompetents. Wendell Berry's novel *Jayber Crow*, which I mentioned earlier, portrays preachers fairly sympathetically. In one instance the young Jayber remarks, "In general, I weathered even the worst sermons pretty well. They had the great virtue of causing my mind to wander. Some of the best things I have ever thought of I have thought of during bad sermons."[22] But good sermons — or even one good sentence in a sermon — can crack open the gospel in a genuinely fresh way. A

22. Berry, *Jayber Crow*, p. 162.

hard human heart is softened, a grieving human spirit comforted, a re-
sistant human heart confronted, a stubborn human mind changed.
Good sermons — and perhaps even bad ones — are powerful tools in
the toolbox of the Holy Spirit.

A survey of the uses of the two short phrases "word of the Lord" and
"word of God" reveals that they appear hundreds of times in the Old Testament and the New Testament. The book of Acts alone contains several
dozen references to the "word of
God" or the "word of the Lord." The
verbs used to describe the people's response to or reception of the word of
God are very diverse. The people "receive" the word; they "believe" it; they
"remember" it; they "desire" it; they
"glorify" it. The apostles "preach" the
word; they "teach" it; they "speak" it.
The word, then, "grows," "increases,"

> There are two types of
> preaching difficult to hear:
> poor preaching and good
> preaching.
>
> Fred Craddock

"multiplies." These verbs cluster around the many sightings of "word of
God" in the book of Acts. Many of these sightings occur within the context of a preaching event. The apostles are preaching the word of God,
and people respond. Clearly, the preached word has enormous power to
reach people, seize them with the truth of the gospel, and cause their
hearts to respond with joy and gratitude. The sermon is the word of God
that presents Jesus Christ in the worship service by the power of the Holy
Spirit.

In a remarkable analogy, J. J. von Allmen suggests that the preacher
is like the Virgin Mary. Like Mary, who "receives, clothes with her substance and gives forth to the world, God's eternal Word," the preacher
receives God's word, clothes it in human words, and proclaims to the
world God's eternal Word.[23] The deep connection between the act of
preaching and the incarnate Word of God, Jesus Christ, is here identi-
fied. Reflecting further on the place of the sermon in the event of worship, Von Allmen dares another analogy: "Despite the aspect of a human

23. Von Allmen, *Worship*, p. 144.

testimony which it also bears, Christian preaching is not simply a meditation on the Word of God. It is a *proclamation* of that Word; it implies a divine miracle."[24]

The sermon as implication of a miracle: this is a description that would occasion a sigh or a raised eyebrow in many faithful church members. If only it were so — that a sermon could imply a miracle. Yet the point that Von Allmen is making has nothing to do with the brilliance, wit, or profundity of the sermon. The sermon is, by its audacious claim to be the word of God for the people at this time in this place, an implication of a miracle. The miracle is a faint but, by God's grace, unmistakable "incarnation" of Jesus Christ. Fully divine, fully human, yet one God-with-us is the Christian confession of the nature of Christ. The sermon dares to make the same claim.

The miracle of the sermon is found in another way as well. The Apostle Paul once compared the preacher to a clay pot (2 Cor. 4:7). Perhaps he was thinking particularly of himself, for he often was seized by self-doubt. To think that the priceless gift of God's grace is stored up in a clay pot, an ordinary human preacher — this is a miracle of God's ingenuity. Preachers who long for more impressive homiletical skills no doubt find the clay-pot image appropriate — too appropriate. How much better, they may think, that God would have chosen to entrust the gospel to grand vases of gilded porcelain — for that might mean that they would have impressive gifts of great rhetorical grandeur and persuasive voices that would stir conversions, stewardship responses, and volunteers for Sunday School teachers. Instead, they are clay pots. My father, a preacher, tells the story of an elderly woman's compliment to him one Sunday morning as he was shaking hands after the service. Grasping his hand earnestly, she looked at him with gratitude and said, "Pastor, thank you for that sermon this morning. The Lord has certainly blessed you with a simple mind." Preachers are clay pots.

The sermon is an implication of a miracle in part because it is a human art form. Those who practice it well know the work involved, the sheer effort to put into frail words, yet once again, the good news of

24. Von Allmen, *Worship*, p. 145.

God's heroic efforts for us and for our salvation. Yet it is also, by the power of the Holy Spirit, the word of God. The Holy Spirit co-opts the words the preacher has put down on the page, the words the preacher has researched, exegeted, pondered, wrestled with, thought over, and puzzled through. The Holy Spirit makes those words the particular word of God for the people of God in gathered worship. A preacher soon learns that the same words fall on different ears in very different ways. Much to her surprise, the preacher even learns that words she has *not* spoken will be reported to her later as being so helpful and instructive. The Spirit is very flexible.

The sermon is the word of God, in a sense, because it makes God "audible" in much the same way that the sacraments make God "visible." First Peter 4:11 puts this thought well: "Whoever speaks must do so as one speaking the very words of God." It is not certain that this verse is referring to preaching, although the context is a discussion of communal gifts such as hospitality, service, and prayer, all of which are to be offered up for the glory of God through Jesus Christ. In this context, "speaking the very words of God" may well be referring to the sermon within the worshiping life of the community.

The Word of God: Sacraments

In some Protestant churches in North America, the communion table and the baptismal font are completely absent in the church. They are simply not present in the worshiping space of the congregation. This is a terrible loss. Among the great treasures of the Christian faith, given to us by God for the nourishment and support of our faith, are the sacraments.[25] The Genevan Reformer John Calvin once remarked, "But as our faith is slight

25. Baptism and the Lord's Supper are the sacraments as recognized in the Protestant traditions. The seven sacraments recognized in the Roman Catholic tradition are Baptism, Confirmation, Eucharist, Reconciliation (Penance), Anointing of the Sick, Marriage, and Holy Orders (Ordination). The six sacraments recognized in the Eastern Orthodox Church are Baptism and Chrismation (Confirmation), Eucharist, Confession, Marriage, Holy Orders, and Anointing of the Sick.

and feeble unless it be propped on all sides and sustained by every means, it trembles, wavers, totters, and at last gives way."[26] Knowing our incurable deficiencies, God, like a tender parent, gives us the gifts of the sacraments, gifts that are perfectly suited to us, gifts that will help support us in all our weaknesses. Calvin will be our guide as we briefly survey the gifts of the sacraments to the church and their connection to the word of God.

Sacraments support and encourage us because they support and encourage the word of God. In fact, the sacraments and the word of God are one; they are united. Calvin attempted to explain this: "For first, the Lord teaches and instructs us by his Word. Secondly, he confirms it by the sacraments. Finally, he illumines our minds by the light of his Holy Spirit and opens our hearts for the Word and sacraments to enter in."[27]

When Calvin says here, "First . . . Secondly . . . Finally," he does not intend any sort of temporal ordering. He is trying to clarify his readers' thinking, trying to organize the importance of the concept. The basic concept is this: through the Holy Spirit, God instructs us by means of both Scripture and sacrament. The sacraments *confirm* what is taught in Scripture. As a matter of fact, the sacraments are a particularly good method of confirming Scripture because we can *see* them. They are *visible* words. We are, remember, tottering fools (Calvin was not one to mince words when it comes to describing our shortcomings), in dire need of all the help we can get. God provides that help by means of the sacraments.

One of Calvin's favorite images of the sacraments is the image of *seals*. The sacraments are like a king's seal on an important government document; it confirms what is written within. Likewise, the sacraments confirm what has been declared in Scripture. There is a unity of Scripture and sacrament. Both are the word of God. Calvin said succinctly, "Therefore, let it be regarded as a settled principle that the sacraments have the same office as the Word of God: to offer and set forth Christ to us, and in him the treasures of heavenly grace."[28]

26. John Calvin, *Institutes of the Christian Religion*, ed. John T. McNeill, trans. Ford Lewis Battles (Philadelphia: Westminster Press, 1960), 4.14.3.

27. Calvin, *Institutes*, 4.14.8.

28. Calvin, *Institutes*, 4.14.17.

In spite of Calvin's "settled principle," he experiments with many metaphors of the sacraments, trying to express the unity of word and sacrament. The sacraments, he says, are like a painting that portrays the promises of God in beautiful visual form. They confirm the promises that God has made. We see them with our eyes, in the water, the bread, the wine. The promises — the water, the bread, the wine — are all one. They are all the word of God.

Or, Calvin says, the sacraments are like great marble pillars. "For as a building stands and rests upon its own foundation but is more surely established by columns placed underneath, so faith rests upon the Word of God as a foundation; but when the sacraments are added, it rests more firmly upon them as upon columns."[29] Faith is the building that depends upon both the foundation of Scripture and the columns of the sacraments. Both are the word of God.

Or, Calvin explains, the sacraments are like mirrors into which we look and contemplate the riches of God's grace. Sacraments are seals, paintings, pillars, mirrors — all intended to support, nourish, grace, and prop up our tottering, feeble faith. This is one of Calvin's contributions to the enormously rich tradition of sacramental theology. The sacraments are a gracious gift of God to the church. Sacraments support the word of God; they are, in fact, united to the word of God. They are united to Scripture; the sacraments support Scripture. And they are united with Christ; the sacraments present Christ to the believing community. In these ways, the sacraments too are the word of God.[30]

Sacraments are a form of the word of God that are given uniquely to the *worshiping community*. Together we celebrate our baptismal identity in worship. The baptismal font should certainly be a visible focal point of worship each and every week. The baptismal font should certainly have water in it each and every week. The story is told that the Reformer Martin Luther fought off the temptations of the devil by growling, "I have been baptized!" For him, this very fact was a powerful part of his identity. Together we also celebrate the feast of Christ's presence in the Lord's

29. Calvin, *Institutes*, 4.14.6.
30. See the chapter "Eucharist ≈ Eschatology" for a fuller exploration of Eucharist.

Supper. It is the food for the journey of Christian discipleship. Calvin says that because God is a most excellent heavenly Father, tenderly concerned for our well-being, God wishes to nourish us, to feed us regularly, with good and healthy food that will sustain us throughout our lives.[31] This is what God gives us in the Lord's Supper. This is why we gather together, in worship, as a big extended family, around the banquet table of God's mercy.

The Word of God: Silence

A long and deep tradition of the church must not be ignored in considering the various ways the Spirit presents Christ to the believer in the word of God. Silent meditation on Scripture is a venerable practice of believers' attentiveness to the revealing grace of the word. In Catholic traditions, silence, meditation, contemplation, and spiritual direction are all aspects of God's self-revelation. Quaker worship practices incorporate silence as a means of listening attentively to God's prompting. Protestant traditions much given to unceasing words are now reclaiming the treasures of these ancient practices. Silence is often practiced in private in a retreat setting, or in the privacy of one's own home. But throughout the Christian tradition, silence has also been a part of gathered worship. Although contemporary culture is deeply allergic to silence, a few seconds of genuine silence are sometimes found. A lovely example is found in the commu-

> Whenever we gather on Sunday, [this] is still our question: Is the Lord among us or not? We thought our problem was the need for freedom, for liberation. No, our problem is thirst. And every Sunday, the preacher strikes the rock, and there is water, things are brought to speech, and silence is broken. The Lord is with us.
>
> William Willimon

31. Calvin, *Institutes*, 4.17.1.

nion liturgy of the Reformed Church in America. After the Sanctus in the Communion Prayer, the rubric in the liturgy calls for a "short period of silence." One of my colleagues imagines, in all holy seriousness, that the reverberations of the angelic choirs in heaven need a few seconds to quiet down before the communion prayer can continue.[32] I like that very much.

The Word of God: Other Forms

Barth is well known for his schema of the threefold form of the Word of God. Other theologians suggest even more. Peter Brunner proposes six forms of the word of God in addition to *the* Word of God, Jesus Christ. They include the reading of Scripture, preaching, the assurance of pardon after the congregation's prayer of confession, the greeting of God spoken at the beginning of the service, the sung psalms and hymns, and the professions of faith in the great creeds of the church.[33] The more extensive list of the forms of the word of God in the worship service is not widely followed by other theologians; the theological conversation tends to follow Barth's threefold scheme of Jesus Christ, Scripture, and preaching, or a twofold scheme of Jesus Christ and Scripture, the Word Incarnate and the word revealed and inspired. The benefit of Brunner's expanded list is that the connections between the word of God and the worship service are imaginatively extended and made concrete. Yes, the word of God is proclaimed in the assurance of pardon. Yes, it is heard in the greeting of God at the beginning of the service and in an excellent hymn text, as well as in the Scripture reading, the sermon, and the sacraments. In all these moments in the worship service, the word of God is proclaimed, Christ is present, and the people of God are united into one body.

32. I owe this insight to Carol Bechtel.

33. Peter Brunner, *Worship in the Name of Jesus*, translated by M. H. Bertram from *Zur Lehre vom Gottesdienst der in Namen Jesu versammelten Gemeinde in Leiturgia: Handbuch des evangelischen Gottesdienstes* (St. Louis: Concordia Publishing House, 1968), pp. 128-41.

How congregations handle all these moments in the worship service will say a great deal about their understanding of the Word of God and their theology of the Word of God. If, for example, a worship service is centered solely on the sermon, with no thoughtful liturgy of God's greeting, no confession and pardon, no clear and well-prepared reading of the Scripture texts, this reflects a theology of the Word that focuses only on the sermon as the "relevant" word of God. Here is a theology of the Word that does not recognize other embodied forms of the word of God or the importance of preparation for a hearing of the word. If, as is the case in many Protestant congregations, the worship service does not include the sacrament of the Lord's Supper each week as a natural response to the sermon, this too has a theological implication. Both sermon and sacrament are meant to "present Christ." Both are meant to nourish believers. They naturally belong together.

The integration of theology and worship has multiple implications. Pull on one thread of worship practices, and theological implications begin to spill out. Pull on one thread of theology, and worship practices begin to spill out. The thoughtful pastor, church leader, and lay person will wish to think through these mutual integrations so that worship and theology can *fit* together and be a fragrant offering to God.

Thanks to God Whose Word Was Spoken

Thanks to God whose word was spoken
in the deed that made the earth;
his the voice that called a nation,
his the fires that tried her worth.
God has spoken,
God has spoken:
praise God for his open word!

Thanks to God whose Word incarnate
human flesh has glorified,
who by life and death and rising
grace abundant has supplied.
God has spoken,
God has spoken:
praise God for his open word!

Thanks to God whose word was written
on the Bible's sacred page,
record of the revelation
showing God to every age.
God has spoken,
God has spoken:
praise God for his open word!

Thanks to God whose word is published
in the tongues of every race;
see its glory undiminished
by the change of time or place.
God is speaking,
God is speaking:
praise God for his open word!

Thanks to God whose word is answered
by the Spirit's voice within;
here we drink of joy unmeasured,
life redeemed from death and sin.
God is speaking,
God is speaking:
praise God for his open word!   *R. T. Brooks (1918-1985), 1954*

Thy Strong Word

Thy strong word did cleave the darkness;
at thy speaking it was done.
For created light we thank thee,
while thine ordered seasons run.
Alleluia! Alleluia!
Praise to thee who light dost send!
Alleluia! Alleluia!
Alleluia without end!

Lo, on those who dwelt in darkness,
dark as night and deep as death,
broke the light of thy salvation,
breathed thine own life-giving breath.
Alleluia! Alleluia!
Praise to thee who light dost send!
Alleluia! Alleluia!
Alleluia without end!

Thy strong Word bespeaks us righteous;
bright with thine own holiness,
glorious now, we press toward glory,
and our lives our hope confess.
Alleluia! Alleluia!
Praise to thee who light dost send!
Alleluia! Alleluia!
Alleluia without end!

From the cross thy wisdom shining
breaketh forth in conquering might;
from the cross forever beameth
all thy bright redeeming light.
Alleluia! Alleluia!
Praise to thee who light dost send!
Alleluia! Alleluia!
Alleluia without end!

Give us lips to sing thy glory,
tongues thy mercy to proclaim,
throats that shout the hope that fills us,
mouths to speak thy holy name.
Alleluia! Alleluia!

May the light which thou dost send
fill our songs with alleluias,
alleluias without end!

God the Father, light-creator,
to thee laud and honor be.
To thee, Light of Light begotten,
praise be sung eternally.
Holy Spirit, light-revealer,
glory, glory be to thee.
Mortals, angels, now and ever
praise the holy Trinity!

Martin H. Franzmann (1907-1979), 1969

Creeds and Prayers | Ecclesiology

Ronald P. Byars

President Dwight Eisenhower once urged Americans, in the 1950s, to have faith in *something*, it didn't much matter what. During that era in particular, the romantic notion flourished that one ought to have faith in faith itself. The early twenty-first century version of that mid-twentieth century notion seems to be faith in "spirituality," which either has no specific reference or is a sort of cafeteria from which the seeker selects a little of this and a little of that. The Russian Orthodox theologian Alexander Schmemann has suggested that a serious contemporary problem is that faith is so often misunderstood as "good feeling." People in our time are not interested in the content of faith "because it is not necessary for [their] 'religiosity,' for that religious feeling that gradually substituted itself for faith and dissolved faith in itself."[1]

Yet the Christian faith does have content. We believe certain things *about* God, *about* human beings, *about* the created world, and *about* their relation. The content of the Christian faith is expressed in creeds. In the worship services of many Christian churches, once Scripture has been read and the sermon preached, the congregation rises together to proclaim the Creed. It does so specifically as a corporate testimony of faith in response to the preached Word. I use the word "proclaim" deliberately. This act is no bare recitation, but public testimony.

---

1. Alexander Schmemann, *The Eucharist: Sacrament of the Kingdom* (Crestwood, N.Y.: St. Vladimir's Seminary Press, 2000), p. 146.

Scriptural Creeds

The corporate proclamation of a common faith has its roots in Scripture
itself. The people of Israel once recited the historical creed that began, "A
wandering Aramean was my ancestor . . ." (Deut. 26:5). Similarly, Psalms
105 and 106 recite the mighty acts of God: "Then Israel came to Egypt. . . .
Then he brought Israel out. . . . He spread a cloud for a covering, and fire
to give light by night. . . . He gave them food from heaven. . . . He gave
them the lands of the nations" (Ps. 105:23, 37, 39, 40, 44). The need for
some sort of common proclamation of God's saving acts in history is
deeply rooted in biblical tradition and continues in the New Testament.
The Apostle Paul may be quoting a credal form familiar to early Christians in the famous *kenosis* passage, which proclaims that "Christ Jesus
. . . though he was in the form of God, did not regard equality with God
as something to be exploited, but emptied himself, taking the form of a
slave . . ." (Phil. 2:6-11). Another example that may have served as a proclamation by the worshiping community is 1 Timothy 3:16: "Without any
doubt, the mystery of our religion is great: He was revealed in flesh, vin-
dicated in spirit, seen by angels, proclaimed among Gentiles, believed in
throughout the world, taken up in glory."

The Nicene Creed

The need for recital of God's redeeming acts by the whole people did
not end in biblical times. The Nicene Creed emerged in the fourth century at a time when the church needed to make a clear statement about
the identity of Jesus Christ. It is traditionally used in Eucharist liturgies.
The Nicene Creed is one of the great ecumenical creeds of the Christian
faith. It is a compact, rich, and dense statement of what Christians have
confessed together over the centuries. Although the language, to some
people, sounds somewhat technical and abstract, its affirmations are
deeply biblical and rooted in a formational piety. Theologian Ellen
Charry reminds us that the Greek word for "of one Being with the Father," the famous word *homoousios*, had a pastoral motive in its original

context.[2] Perhaps the stately language of the Nicene Creed can serve as a needed reminder to us, who are tempted to chase after the "new and now," that we have been shaped by the witness of those who have gone before us and by the Spirit of God, who has guided the church and continues to guide us today.

The text of the Nicene Creed is as follows:

> We believe in one God,
> the Father, the Almighty,
> maker of heaven and earth,
> of all that is, seen and unseen.
>
> We believe in one Lord, Jesus Christ,
> the only Son of God,
> eternally begotten of the Father,
> God from God, Light from Light,
> true God from true God,
> begotten, not made,
> of one Being with the Father;
> through him all things were made.
> For us and for our salvation
> he came down from heaven,
> was incarnate of the Holy Spirit and the Virgin Mary
> and became truly human.
> For our sake he was crucified under Pontius Pilate;
> he suffered death and was buried.
> On the third day he rose again
> in accordance with the Scriptures;
> he ascended into heaven

2. The formation of the Nicene Creed was also, of course, politically and polemically complex. Ellen Charry's point is that the impulse of patristic theology was deeply "aretegenic" or pastorally motivated. The great champion of the *homoousios*, Athanasius, understood this term to be an instruction for the community toward the kind of unity that characterizes the Father and the Son. See *By the Renewing of Your Minds* (Oxford: Oxford University Press, 1997), p. 97.

and is seated at the right hand of the Father.
He will come again in glory to judge the living and the dead,
and his kingdom will have no end.

We believe in the Holy Spirit, the Lord, the giver of life,
who proceeds from the Father and the Son,
who with the Father and the Son is worshiped and glorified,
who has spoken through the prophets.
We believe in one holy catholic and apostolic church.
We acknowledge one baptism for the forgiveness of sin.
We look for the resurrection of the dead,
and the life of the world to come. Amen.[3]

Why Recite a Creed?

The liturgical use of the Creed is an uncomfortable moment for many
North American Christians because most of us live with an underdevel-
oped ecclesiology — that is, an insufficient doctrine of the church. Some
people have the mistaken idea that the Creed is meant to articulate the
faith of individual persons. They think that if they say the Creed aloud,
they must know what it fully means and they must fully agree with it.
Anything short of this constitutes personal perjury. But this idea betrays
a mistaken understanding of the church.

Visitors to North America in centuries past have taken note of the
American affection for choosing to belong to private associations of
various sorts, but the church is fundamentally different from a club, a
class, or even those committed to sharing the faith with one another. In
New Testament terms, the church is part of the gospel, not an add-on. To
be in Christ means to be in the body of Christ, the church. One is not
possible without the other.

3. This text is the English translation of the Nicene Creed prepared by the English
Language Liturgical Consultation (ELLC). Copyright © 1988, ELLC. All rights reserved.
This translation can be found in *Praying Together* (Nashville: Abingdon Press, 1988).

The work (*leitourgia* or *liturgy*) of the church includes the gathering of the baptized *all together* in one place around the Word and the shared sacramental Meal. The church, with its faults and its collection of diverse and sometimes incompatible personalities, is sometimes difficult, but taking responsibility for being a part of the church is part of the believer's calling. The Spirit gives us strength for taking that responsibility as we gather together as the church to praise, confess, hear the Word, proclaim our faith, lament, make our petitions to God, and eat and drink with the risen Lord.

Our deep individualism makes all this *togetherness* hard for us. There is something in the history and culture of the United States that sets individuals against groups. In colonial times, it was colonists over against the authority of Britain. Then it was states over against the authority of a central government. This "over-againstness" is understandable in terms of American history. The first Americans were refugees from various kinds of oppression. Subsequent immigration has brought to our society other waves of people in search of one kind of liberty or another.

While people of the United States form all sorts of groups eagerly and easily, we tend to leave them as easily as we form them. In terms of American culture, the ultimate authority is the individual. Garrison Keillor told the story of a man who had been marooned on a desert island. After some years, he was discovered. When his rescuers arrived on shore, the marooned man offered to show them around the island he had made his home. He showed them a house he had built out of driftwood. He showed them a little office he had erected from the branches of trees. Finally, with great pride, he showed them a little building with a cross on top, saying, "This is my church!" His rescuers, noticing another

> God wants to be thought of as our Lover. I must see myself so bound in love as if everything that has been done has been done for me. That is to say, the Love of God makes such a unity in us that when we see this unity no one is able to separate oneself from another.
>
> Julian of Norwich

building with a cross, asked him about it. "That's the church I *used* to go to," he replied.

In the United States, the fact that no one is obligated to join any religious organization has proven to strengthen the church. Nevertheless, it has been easy to construe the church as just another civic or social organization, not unlike the service clubs that meet weekly for lunch, open with prayer and singing, provide a stimulating speaker, and take up a collection for a community project. When the church is conceived simply as a voluntary organization, an affiliation one makes for the sake of companionship in faith, or mutual reinforcement, or finding allies in the service of a common cause, one wears the relationship lightly. When one church doesn't serve me or my cause as well as I had hoped, it is easy to leave it, or to join some other church that promises to do a better job of meeting my needs. If I don't like the Creed, it is just as easy to find a church that has a creed more to my taste. It is not surprising, then, that in the kind of culture which has grown out of the American experience, the church has not been understood as having any but the most modest claim on its members, and the faith of the church can easily be misunderstood as simply the majority view of the individuals who belong to it.

Kathleen Norris tells the story of an Orthodox theologian who was a visiting lecturer in a seminary classroom, speaking about the historical development of the creeds. A student in the class asked a question that produced an illuminating exchange:

> "What can one do when one finds it impossible to affirm certain tenets of the Creed?" [The student's question may have been, in other words, "May I stand politely, but silently, while the congregation recites the Creed? Or shall I say aloud only those lines that I'm sure I believe?"] The priest responded, "Well, you just say it. It's not that hard to master. With a little effort, most can learn it by heart."
>
> . . . The student, apparently feeling that he had been misunderstood, asked with some exasperation, "What am I to do . . . when I have difficulty affirming parts of the Creed . . . ?" And he got the same response. "You just say it. Particularly when you have difficulty believing it. . . ."

The student raised his voice: "How can I with integrity affirm a creed which I do not believe?" And the priest replied, "It's not your creed, it's our creed," meaning the Creed of the entire Christian church. . . . "Eventually it may come to you," he told the student. "For some, it takes longer than for others. . . ."[4]

The crucial point is exactly this: the Creed is not the possession of any single individual; it belongs to the church catholic, to the covenanted community, called and chosen at God's initiative. "It's our creed." As individuals, any one of us would likely choose to articulate the doctrinal content of our faith in words that are particularly appropriate to us. We would choose words that express our experience, our history, our particular ways of speaking. But when the church is summoned to rise and profess its common faith, it does so not in a cacophony of simultaneous personal testimonies, but in words that belong to the community of saints, including both the living and the dead.

Just as we do not each invent our own words to the hymns we sing in church but sing texts that express faith, perhaps, quite differently than we would do if left to our own devices, we profess the faith of the church with one voice because we are a part of the church. It may be that, with respect to the faith, we are among those members whom impartial observers might describe as mature; or it may be that we are among the less mature. The Creed represents the faith of the church — the faith with which, mature or immature, we have to do. If, for now, these affirmations seem beyond us, we continue to say them nevertheless. They are not our words but the church's. Our work is to say them until we grow into them. Eventually it may come to us. "For some, it takes longer than for others."

That does not mean that we are to swallow our questions or stifle our dissent. It does mean that the purpose of our questioning and the purpose even of our dissent is that we shall grow to the point where we embrace this faith and internalize it rather than too hastily writing it off

4. Kathleen Norris, *Amazing Grace: A Vocabulary of Faith* (New York: Riverhead Books, 1998), pp. 64-65.

because it is alien to the contemporary mind. When we grow into the church's faith, we reserve the right to understand it differently than some others may understand it, as well as the right to understand it differently than when we first encountered it. The Creed remains, however, a verbal expression of the church's faith, with all the limitations that implies, but nevertheless rightfully claiming our respectful attention and lifelong reflection.

Rather than falling silent to avoid this or that affirmation, one might resolve to trust the possibility that the church (or, at least, some voices in the great church) might mentor us faithfully — even through affirmations that are difficult for us — if we will permit ourselves to take the humble role of apprentice. "For some, it takes longer than for others. . . ." One congregation always follows the proclamation of the Creed with a brief prayer in which everyone joins, from those whose faith is most confident to those whose hold on faith is the most tenuous. The prayer centers on the words of Scripture in which a man, seeking help for a child in trouble, cries out to Jesus, "Lord, I believe; help my unbelief!" (Mark 9:24). We believe, Lord. Help our unbelief.

In that vacillation between belief and unbelief, the church can play a supportive role. John Calvin used a simile different from that of mentor and apprentice. He wrote of the church as our mother. "For there is no other way to enter into life unless this mother conceive us in her womb, give us birth, nourish us at her breast, and lastly, unless she keep us under her care and guidance until, putting off mortal flesh, we become like the angels."[5]

Similarly, a familiar African proverb states, "It takes a whole village to raise a child." In other words, communities shape persons. With their long and extensive experience, with wisdom accumulated in debate and even conflict, in the very substance of their shared life, communities form the way that novices perceive reality and name it. There is a reality

5. John Calvin, *Institutes of the Christian Religion*, ed. John T. McNeill, trans. Ford Lewis Battles (Philadelphia: Westminster Press, 1960), 4.1.4. Here Calvin echoes Augustine, who said, "This is the Church which, imitating his [Christ's] mother, daily gives birth to his members yet remains virgin." See *Enchiridion* X.34, in *Augustine: Confessions and Enchiridion*, ed. Albert C. Outler (Philadelphia: Westminster Press, 1955), p. 360.

to corporate life that is other than the sum total of individual experiences, thoughts, and convictions. So it is with the church. The ecumenical church, whose faith is represented in the Nicene Creed, has a mentoring role, a mothering role, a formative role that precedes the faith of its individual members while both expecting and enabling the development of personal faith.

When we stand as a community of faith to recite the Creed in its precise and spare verbal statements, it may seem to some people to be an exercise of the intellect. The Protestant Reformers of the sixteenth century perhaps understood how a verbal recitation might lead to such a misunderstanding, because both Luther and Calvin provided for the singing of the Creed in worship — for Luther's liturgy, it was the Nicene Creed, and for Calvin's, the Apostles' Creed.[6] An English version of Luther's sung Creed is "We All Believe in One True God."[7]

> We all believe in one true God,
> who created earth and heaven,
> the Father, who to us in love
> has the right of children given.
> He in soul and body feeds us;
> all we need his hand provides us;
> through all snares and perils leads us.
> Watching that no harm betide us,
> he cares for us by day and night.
> All things are governed by his might.

6. Bard Thompson, *Liturgies of the Western Church* (Philadelphia: Fortress Press, 1961), p. 132. Calvin used a sung version of the Apostles' Creed in the French liturgy of Strasbourg (1540) and Geneva liturgy (1542). See Thompson, p. 306 n. 9.

7. "We All Believe in One True God," *Lutheran Book of Worship* (Minneapolis: Augsburg Fortress, 1978), no. 374. Translation from *The Lutheran Hymnal*, 1941. Copyright © 1941 Concordia Publishing House. Used by permission.

Simpler versions of this hymn may be found in *The Presbyterian Hymnal* (Louisville: Westminster/John Knox Press, 1990), no. 137, and in *The United Methodist Hymnal* (Nashville: United Methodist Publishing House, 1989), no. 85.

We all believe in Jesus Christ,
his own Son, our Lord, possessing
an equal Godhead, throne, and might,
source of every grace and blessing;
born of Mary, virgin mother,
by the power of the Spirit,
Word made flesh, our elder brother;
that the lost might life inherit,
was put to death upon the cross,
and raised by God victorious.

We all confess the Holy Ghost,
who, in highest heaven dwelling
with God the Father and the Son,
comforts us beyond all telling;
who the church, his own creation,
keeps in unity of spirit.
Here forgiveness and salvation
daily come through Jesus' merit.
All flesh shall rise, and we shall be
in bliss with God eternally.

The Apostles' Creed

Persons become members of the church not because they have already mastered the faith, understand it perfectly, and have successfully incorporated the practice of it into their daily lives. Persons are made members of the church by baptism. In early generations, persons typically approached the church because they had been impressed (believe it or not!) by the character of its members. The question put to those whose inquiry led to their request to be enrolled in the catechumenate was "What do you ask of God's church?" The prospective catechumen's answer was "Faith." In the course of preparing catechumens for baptism, the church "handed over" to them (the Latin word comes from *traditio*, obviously the root of our "tradition") early versions of what we call the Apostles' Creed. This handing over provided the catechumens with an outline of the received content of the Christian faith. At the time of their baptism, the catechumens "handed" it back *(redditio)*, making personal affirmation in the words of the church.

Whether infant, child, adolescent, or mature adult, those who come to be baptized come not because they already have faith — or at least not a mature faith. They come to a beginning point meant to lead to the fullness of a deep and vigorous faith. In baptism, they are at the starting line. Their incorporation into Christ and the church marks the inauguration of a lifelong formation, not separate from but within the community of faith. Unlike the ancient mystery religions and ancient Jewish practice, in which adherents seeking ritual purity baptized (washed) themselves, in Christian baptism, a minister baptizes. In sharp contrast to known custom (both Jewish and non-Jewish) in the first century, the act of one person baptizing another signified a gift given. Faith was not something one reached out independently to take possession of, but something given as a gift to the one who came to the community in search of it. Faith in the triune God characterized the community, and that faith was handed on *(traditio)* to those who wanted to grow into it.

The Apostles' Creed, in various forms, became associated with baptism in the churches of the West. It evolved from the early centuries of the church, traditionally from apostolic roots. Although it was not penned by the apostles themselves, the Creed's simple biblical narrative gives it a structure and a nontechnical simplicity and freshness that have endeared it to centuries of Christian believers and embedded it in baptismal liturgies. Schleiermacher de-

> And those who enter the church are clothed in a white garment. Some of them rejoice with great joy in the smoothness and softness of this garment, and keep it on. But others seem bothered by its weight and confining nature, and try to take it off.
>
> Hildegard of Bingen

scribes it as "a brief compendium of doctrine based on Scripture."[8] Drawn line by line from Scripture, the Apostles' Creed represents the faith handed on to the new converts. Sometimes called simply the "Symbol," or "the rule of faith," it lays out the basic structure of the biblical faith as Christians have received it. In its contemporary form, in the version provided by the International Commission on English in the Liturgy, the Apostles' Creed, like the Nicene Creed, follows a Trinitarian form:

I believe in God, the Father almighty,
creator of heaven and earth.

I believe in Jesus Christ, God's only Son, our Lord,
who was conceived by the Holy Spirit,
born of the Virgin Mary,
suffered under Pontius Pilate,
was crucified, died, and was buried;
he descended to the dead.
On the third day he rose again;
he ascended into heaven,
he is seated at the right hand of the Father,
and he will come again to judge the living and the dead.

I believe in the Holy Spirit,
the holy catholic church,
the communion of saints,
the forgiveness of sins,
the resurrection of the body,
and the life everlasting. Amen.[9]

8. Friedrich Schleiermacher, *The Christian Faith* (Edinburgh: T&T Clark, 1960), p. 617.

9. This text is the English translation of the Apostles' Creed prepared by the English Language Liturgical Consultation (ELLC). Copyright © 1988, ELLC. All rights reserved. This translation can be found in *Praying Together* (Nashville: Abingdon Press, 1988).

When the congregation sings the Creed, everyone senses that the point of it is doxological rather than argumentative. It is not an intellectual exercise but the celebration of a faith that rests ultimately in the triune God, whom the church identifies and proclaims by means of these fragile, yet bold, words.

The Prayers of the People

The people who respond to the Word in a doxological proclamation of the church's faith in the creeds also come before God in the Prayers of the People. Although, in most cases, only one person, usually the minister or liturgist, will voice the Prayers of the People, the prayers are framed in the first-person plural "we" rather than the first-person singular "I." That person speaks on behalf of all, and the "Amen" belongs to all the people: "So be it!"

The Prayers of the People have their roots in Jewish prayer both in the Temple and in the synagogue. While first-century sources are sketchy, the patterns of synagogue worship in the first century can be patched together from information in the Mishna,[10] dating from the second century.[11] The Amidah, or Eighteen Benedictions, formed an important part of the synagogue liturgy. It began with three benedictions of praise and concluded with three benedictions of thanksgiving. In between were six petitions, which were at first somewhat fluid, taking the form of supplications, and six intercessions. It may be that the Lord's Prayer, which Jesus taught his disciples, is a shortened version of the Amidah.[12] It is significant to note that in the gospel Jesus redirected the scope of his disciples' prayers. Revising traditional Jewish liturgical practice, he specifically instructed his disciples to pray for their enemies:

10. The Mishnah is a collection of scriptural interpretations; for Jews it is second in authority only to the scripture.

11. Frank C. Senn, *Christian Liturgy: Catholic and Evangelical* (Minneapolis: Fortress Press, 1997), pp. 68ff.

12. Hughes Oliphant Old, *Worship That Is Reformed According to Scripture* (Atlanta: John Knox Press, 1984), p. 94.

"You have heard that it was said, 'You shall love your neighbor and hate your enemy.' But I say to you, Love your enemies and pray for those who persecute you" (Matt. 5:43-44). Prayer for enemies and persecutors goes beyond the boundaries of the Amidah, which included no petitions for those outside Israel, although such prayer would seem a logical extension of the vocation of the people of God, in whom "all the families of the earth shall be blessed."

Prayer Reaching Outside the Walls

The early church seems to have taken Jesus' instructions seriously. In the First Letter to Timothy, these are the directions for the church's prayers: "First of all, then, I urge that supplications, prayers, intercessions, and thanksgivings be made for everyone, for kings and all who are in high positions" (1 Tim. 2:1-2). The church is to pray for *everyone* — including the secular authorities, who were certainly not, in that period, members of the church.

> Traditionalism is the dead faith of the living. Tradition is the living faith of the dead.
>
> Jaroslav Pelikan

The Epistle of Clement (about A.D. 90) declares that the assembly offers prayer for the civil authorities as well as for leaders of the church. The Epistle provides "a list of intercessions for the afflicted, the fallen, the needy, the sick, the wandering, prisoners, and the salvation of all nations." It then "asks for mercy to those who have sinned and peace 'for us and to all that dwell on the earth.'"[13] *The Clementine Liturgy,* dating from the end of the fourth century, includes extensive prayers of intercession, beginning, "Let us pray for the peace and welfare of the world . . ." and continuing with prayers for the church and various of its officers and members, for the sick, for those who travel, for those who are imprisoned or in exile, for those in slavery, and for enemies, "those who hate

13. Old, *Worship That Is Reformed According to Scripture,* p. 96.

us," and "those who persecute us on account of the name of the Lord."[14]
This pattern of offering intercessions for those outside the church is well
attested throughout the early centuries. It began to fade in the Middle
Ages, and by the end of that period it had been reduced to a vestigial re-
mainder in the Roman mass.

At the Reformation, Martin Bucer's Strasbourg Liturgy recovered
the Prayer of Intercession, similar in pattern to those of the early centuries. The Strasbourg Liturgy included prayers for "our lord Emperor and
King, all princes and nobles, and the magistrates and ruling body of this
city," and acknowledged that the Lord Jesus Christ "hast commanded us
to petition thee for all men."[15] John Calvin's *The Form of Church Prayers* followed Bucer's model, as did Thomas Cranmer's *Book of Common Prayer*.[16]

Ministers led most of the service from the pulpit during the Reformation. The reason for this was practical rather than liturgical. In the
medieval mass, it was not important for the people to hear the words of
the priest. In the churches of the Reformation, it was very important.
When ministers led the whole service from the pulpit, it was in order
that the prayers be heard. Today, because of sound amplification sys-
tems, it is not necessary to lead the entire service from the pulpit. In fact,
to move as appropriate to Table or Font makes a visual statement about
the meaning of the liturgical acts led from those places. The Prayers of
the People might appropriately be led from the Table, or the one leading
these prayers might stand in the midst of the congregation. In either
case, the visual symbolism is that we have turned toward God in prayer.

The Components of Prayer

A mnemonic device some have used to remember the necessary prayers
of the Lord's Day assembly is A-C-T-S — Adoration, Confession,

14. R. H. Cresswell, *The Liturgy of the Eighth Book of 'The Apostolic Constitutions' Commonly Called The Clementine Liturgy* (London: Society for Promoting Christian Knowledge;
New York: The Macmillan Co., 1900), pp. 46-49.

15. Thompson, *Liturgies of the Western Church*, pp. 172-73.

16. Thompson, *Liturgies of the Western Church*, p. 200 and pp. 256ff.

Thanksgiving, and Supplication. In some churches, virtually all of the major prayers of the service are concentrated in one long prayer, often called the "Pastoral Prayer." In other liturgies, prayers are distributed throughout the service, situated in the contexts most appropriate to the theological themes they represent.

Adoration and Confession

In most contemporary liturgies, quite typically the opening of the service will call for a prayer focusing on praise or adoration. It's not that God needs to be flattered, but planted deep within human beings is a need to express praise for that which is great, and good, and beautiful. Gathered before the Holy One, the congregation's first corporate act is to bless God.

Like Isaiah, who was moved to confession when he saw a vision of God in the Temple (Isa. 6:1-8), those who find themselves standing before the greatness of God may be moved to humility. The prayer of confession, offered in many liturgies near the opening of the service, and in some liturgies just preceding the Eucharist, not only brings before God the brokenness of those present, but also confesses the sins of the whole church and of the entire world. The confession of sin is akin to the psalms of lament, in which the church boldly, and with confidence in the graciousness of God, cries out its own need for healing for ourselves, for all the baptized, for every human being, every creature, and for the created world itself.

Thanksgiving — and Lament, the Forgotten Prayer

Prayers of thanksgiving occur at several times during the worship service. Many of the opening sentences, such as "Our help is in the name of the Lord, who made heaven and earth" and "This is the day that the Lord has made — let us rejoice and be glad in it" are themselves, implicitly, prayers of thanksgiving. The prayer after the offering has been taken is a prayer of thanksgiving and dedication. Often, prayers of thanksgiving appear in hymn texts.

A central prayer of thanksgiving in the service is the Eucharistic prayer, the Great Thanksgiving over the bread and cup. This prayer begins with these familiar words: "The Lord be with you. *And also with you. Lift up your hearts. We lift them up to the Lord.* Let us give thanks to the Lord our God. *It is right to give our thanks and praise."*

Rooted in Jewish ways of praying, the Great Thanksgiving evolved as a prayer in which the church remembers God's mighty acts and gives thanks for them, and recalls in particular the incarnation, life, death, resurrection, and ascension of Christ. We also pray for the Holy Spirit to bless us and the gifts of bread and wine, to make manifest the body of Christ to us as we wait in hope and confidence for Christ's coming in glory and the consummation of all things.

Giving thanks to God for our joys and blessings is an important part of Christian worship and faithful Christian devotion. But it is not complete. The sorrows and griefs of life are also brought to God in prayer. Lament, too, is an important aspect of Christian prayer. A member of one congregation complained that it made him feel depressed when we prayed for someone who was sick or another who was bereaved. It may be true that many people don't want to be reminded that there is heartache, injustice, and loss in this world; and perhaps some of those people come to church with the expectation of escaping the stress and pain of daily life.

> The Christian church has a language, and her creeds teach it to us. . . . This is a language that is always old and always new. Jesus teaches us to love the Lord our God with all our mind. For us to learn how to "talk Christian" shows not just that we are good students. It also shows we are good lovers.
>
> Cornelius Plantinga Jr.

Our prayer is praise and thanksgiving — which some might call "upbeat" — but juxtaposed to it is also our lamentation. In his letter to the Romans, the Apostle instructs, "Rejoice with those who rejoice, weep with those who weep" (Rom. 12:15). Where there is only lamentation, and no praise and thanksgiving, something is out of balance, and there is justification for feeling depressed. When there is only praise and thanksgiving, we have lifted off of the earth and turned our backs on it in order to preserve an artificial sense of well-being. The church's prayer is not a form of hypnosis or false therapy. It is standing with and alongside all the families of the earth, crying out to God on their behalf, in gratitude for the magnificent blessings all enjoy, and in lamentation that in this world, people get hurt.

In their book *Rachel's Cry: Prayer of Lament and Rebirth of Hope*, Daniel Migliore and Kathleen Billman note that prayers of lament are often not given room in the worship service. "As a result, instead of providing space for protest and grief, what churches often offer are worship services that are 'unrelentingly positive in tone.'"[17] Billman and Migliore are convinced that the biblical tradition of the psalms of lament and other prayers of lament in Scripture can lead Christian believers today back to a more whole and balanced expression of Christian faith. The prayers of lament have been "exiled" from much contemporary Christian worship. It is time to bring lament back into the worship service. These authors ask:

> How can praise be free and joyful if the realities of broken human life are not named and lamented? How can heartfelt thanks be given for healing if the wounds are denied? How can confession of sin be sincere if we turn all sorrow into guilt? How can intercession be strong if our language does not reflect knowledge of the real sufferings of those for whom we pray?[18]

Prayers of lament do not end in the worship service. They do not stay within the walls of the church. Lament finds its way into efforts for justice and reconciliation. Lament finds its way into ministries of care. Many congregations are actively involved with various forms of ministry in the community. Some congregations are building Habitat houses

---

17. Kathleen Billman and Daniel L. Migliore, *Rachel's Cry: Prayer of Lament and Rebirth of Hope* (Cleveland: United Church Press, 1999), p. 14. Quote from Elaine Ramshaw, *Ritual and Pastoral Care* (Philadelphia: Fortress Press, 1987), pp. 31-32.

18. Billman and Migliore, *Rachel's Cry*, p. 19.

for families who need adequate housing. Others provide meals or shelter for the homeless. Almost all make some provision for members of the church — not just pastors — to provide care for congregational members who are sick, hospitalized, or bereaved. Perhaps a person involved in one of those ministries might be invited to lead the Prayers of the People from time to time. The man who has taken a week or two of his annual vacation to organize volunteers on a Habitat project, or a parish nurse, or a member of a care committee, or someone who organizes meals for bereaved families can lead the prayers and simply by their visible presence send a clear message to the congregation that there is a profound link between their priesthood within the sanctuary and their priesthood outside it.

All is not as we would have it be. Our solidarity with the suffering is our burden to bear, but it is also our true vocation. Don Saliers says, "To join Christ in his ongoing prayer for the world is to be plunged more deeply into the densities of social reality, not to be taken out of them."[19] The burden is not ours alone: our great High Priest shares its weight. "Consequently he is able for all time to save those who approach God through him, since he always lives to make intercession for them" (Heb. 7:25).

Supplication

The church intercedes on behalf of the whole broken world and all its families, those who pray for themselves and those who don't, those who can't pray for themselves and those who won't. That intercession becomes concrete in terms of the church's ministry and mission directed toward those outside the church. The church may be an advocate for the powerless, a voice for the voiceless, drawing attention to those who are left out or forgotten, or whose pleas for justice or compassion have been overlooked by the larger society. In its worship, the church continually rehearses its role as intercessor, particularly in the Prayers

---

19. Don Saliers, *Worship as Theology: Foretaste of Glory Divine* (Nashville: Abingdon Press, 1994), pp. 126-27.

of the People. As we pray for those who are religiously, politically, and economically different from us — even at odds with us — we engage in a kind of reprogramming to exorcise our prejudices. In effect, we petition God to reshape our minds and hearts so that those whom we might easily regard as enemies may become visible to us as precious in God's sight. There is, no doubt, wisdom in the practice of Temple, synagogue, and early church, in which there were more or less fixed patterns of intercession. When our prayer is shaped entirely by local concerns or concerns of the moment, it is easy to skip over the hard praying and pray only for ourselves, those with whom we are acquainted, and others like us.

> Conversion doesn't offer a form of knowledge that can be bought and sold, quantified, or neatly packaged. It is best learned slowly and in community, the way a Native American child learns his or her traditional religion, the way an adult learns to be a Benedictine, not by book learning or weekend workshops but by being present at the ceremonies. Truly present, with a quiet heart that allows you to become a good listener, an observer of those — plants, animals, cloud formations, people, and words — who know and define the territory.
>
> Kathleen Norris

Over the generations, the church has learned something about the breadth of its intercessory priesthood. Prayers include petitions for the church itself, its ministry and those who minister; for the local congregation; for the nations and those in authority; for peace and justice in the world; for the earth and a right use of its resources; for the community and those who govern; for the poor and the oppressed; for the sick, the bereaved, the lonely — all who suffer in body, mind, or spirit; and for those with special needs.[20] Karl Barth's well-known suggestion that one should preach with the Bible in one hand and

---

20. See the *Book of Common Worship* (Louisville: Westminster/ John Knox Press, 1993), p. 99.

the newspaper in the other applies with at least equal force to the church's prayers. The sermon may or may not address some pressing issue in society, but the Prayers of the People will always hold up before God whatever brokenness in the world has come to our attention. We pray for victims of natural disasters, disease, warfare, and conflict, for the homeless, and for ourselves.

When the church prays, it not only lifts up the immediate needs of the world but does so in anticipation of God's new creation, the reign of God (the kingdom of God). In the Lord's Prayer, the church prays, "Thy kingdom come, Thy will be done, on earth as it is in heaven." That kingdom is not yet fully here, but it nevertheless manifests itself among us now and then. Scripture offers a picture of it, and we catch a glimpse of it now here, now there. Isaiah helps us know what to look for. "They shall beat their swords into plowshares, and their spears into pruning hooks; nation shall not lift up sword against nation, neither shall they learn war any more" (Isa. 2:4). "The wolf shall live with the lamb, the leopard shall lie down with the kid. . . . The nursing child shall play over the hole of the asp. . . . They will not hurt or destroy on all my holy mountain; for the earth will be full of the knowledge of the LORD as the waters cover the sea" (Isa. 11:6, 8, 9). "Then the glory of the LORD shall be revealed, and all people shall see it together" (Isa. 40:5). In the praise, thanksgiving, and intercessions of the church, we anticipate the healing of the whole creation, celebrate any sign of its appearance among us, and ask God to manifest that healing in the world now, and to empower us to be agents of that healing. Our prayer is rooted in the faith of the church.

Faith, according to the Epistle to the Hebrews, "is the assurance of things hoped for, the conviction of things not seen" (Heb. 11:1). According to Alexander Schmemann, our faith "manifests and . . . grants that to which it is directed: the presence among us of the approaching kingdom of God and its unfading light."[21] In its prayers for others, the church, in faith, affirms its eschatological hope.

It is not surprising that when the congregation is regularly invited to make prayer requests, the time devoted to intercessory prayer becomes

21. Schmemann, *The Eucharist*, p. 35.

longer rather than shorter. This happens because people come to church with many concerns on their minds, and those concerns are not exclusively for themselves. In a congregation that offered people the opportunity to write down their prayer concerns, there were many requests for prayer for colleagues at work, for neighbors not members of that church (or of any church), for people whose plights had become public in newspaper or television news stories, as well as for other members of the congregation. People also wanted prayers for those who live on the streets, for those devastated by hurricanes or floods, and for those who find themselves in the path of conflict in various parts of the world.

Lord, Hear Our Prayer!

The traditional Pastoral Prayer tries to steer between two dangers: being too long for the congregation to maintain its focus, or being too short, though it was deliberately made short in an effort to spare the congregation the need to be attentive to an unrelieved flood of words. Many contemporary service books offer ways of inviting the congregation to participate in the Prayers of the People. When the prayers are divided into smaller portions, to which the congregation responds with a sung or spoken response, it is easier for the people to remain engaged with the prayers, especially if they have had an opportunity to identify persons or situations to be included in the prayers. After each petition, the one leading the prayer may end with "In your mercy, Lord . . . ," or "Gracious God, in your mercy . . . ," to which the people can respond, "Hear our prayer." Or each petition may be ended with "through Jesus Christ our Lord," to which the people add their "Amen," sung or spoken.

In one congregation, after each petition the leader says, "In your mercy, Lord . . . ," after which a handbell strikes a tone, and all sing a short chant from the Taizé community in France: "Jesus, remember me when you come into your kingdom."[22] Another sung response might

22. *Taizé: Songs for Prayer* (Chicago: GIA Publications, Inc., 1998), no. 11. This is also available in some denominational hymnals, such as *The Presbyterian Hymnal*, no. 599.

be a chant from the Iona Community in Scotland: "Lord Jesus Christ, Lover of all, fling wide the hem of your garment; bring healing, bring peace."[23] The oldest such response is the *Kyrie Eleison* ("Lord, have mercy"), the only piece of the liturgy still in the Greek language, dating from before the Latin mass. There are many forms of the Kyrie, including several versions created to be sung in the prayers of intercession in the Taizé and Iona services, as well as settings in many denominational hymnals.

The Prayers of the People need not be tedious. In fact, they may constitute the part of the service that the congregation most anticipates. When the one leading stands in the midst of the congregation, the people might be invited to stand and face one another across the aisle. Standing for prayer is uncomfortable if it requires bowing the head and closing the eyes. Such a posture implies humility, but it also resembles a kind of closing up within oneself (not to mention that for some it poses the problem of keeping their balance). Jewish worshipers in Jesus' time were more likely to stand with hands outstretched and faces uplifted. In the early church, Christian congregations stood for prayer. For centuries they persisted in the use of this posture for prayer. A contemporary congregation might be willing at least to stand, with heads unbowed, in a posture that more nearly resembles openness both to God and to neighbor than a more closed position does.

Silence plays a role in our prayers as well. Twenty-first-century people are not very patient with silence, often perceiving it as nothing more than empty time. However, silence need not be simply the absence of sound. Silence is an opportunity in worship for God to speak a word of comfort or challenge, a word of instruction or insight or warning, a word of gracious consolation or tender mercy. Silence can even be lengthy. At the Taizé community in France, which draws thousands of young people to its worship, I once timed a silence at fifteen minutes, and yet it was a pregnant silence, a vivid silence.

The Creed and the Prayers of the People help to form us as the

23. John L. Bell and Graham Maule, *Wild Goose Songs*, vol. 1: *Heaven Shall Not Wait*, rev. ed. (Glasgow: Wild Goose Publications, 1989), p. 119.

church. The word "ecclesiastical" has its origin in the Greek word ἐκκλησία (ἐκ καλέω — "called out"). In Trinitarian language, God the Father has called out a people, through Christ, by the power of the Holy Spirit. "You did not choose me but I chose you" (John 15:16). By God's intent and purpose, Christ is the head of the church, and the Holy Spirit is the source of its vitality. It is faith in this God that we proclaim doxologically in the ecumenical creeds. It is this very God who has chosen us to be a royal priesthood in the world — which priesthood we rehearse in our communal prayers and exercise in society. The object of the church's corporate priesthood is the whole world — "all the families of the earth." In our prayer we bless God, and in our priesthood, God works in us, through us, and sometimes in spite of us to bless God's creation, all against the horizon of God's ultimate sovereign rule, the eschatological consummation in which that blessing shall reach its completion.

O Christ, the Great Foundation

O Christ, the great foundation
on which your people stand
to preach your true salvation
in every age and land,
pour out your Holy Spirit
to make us strong and pure,
to keep the faith unbroken
as long as worlds endure.

Baptized in one confession,
one church in all the earth,
we bear our Lord's impression,
the sign of second birth.
One holy people gathered
in love beyond our own.
By grace we were invited;
by grace we make you known.

Where tyrants' hold is tightened,
where strong devour the weak,
where innocents are frightened,
the righteous fear to speak,
there let your church awaking
attack the powers of sin,
and, all their ramparts breaking,
with you the victory win.

This is the moment glorious
when he who once was dead
shall lead his church victorious,
their champion and their head.
The Lord of all creation
his heavenly kingdom brings,
the final consummation,
the glory of all things.

Timothy T'ingfang Lew (1892-1947), Chinese, 1933;
trans. Mildred A. Wiant (1898-2001), 1966

Our Cities Cry to You, O God

Our cities cry to you, O God,
from out their pain and strife;
you made us for yourself alone,
but we choose alien life.
Our goals are pleasure, gold, and power;
injustice stalks our earth;
in vain we seek for rest, for joy,
for sense of human worth.

Yet still you walk our streets, O Christ!
We know your presence here
where humble Christians love and serve
in godly grace and fear.
O Word made flesh, be seen in us!
May all we say and do
affirm you God Incarnate still
and turn sad hearts to you!

Your people are your hands and feet
to serve your world today;
our lives the book our cities read
to help them find your way.
O pour your sovereign Spirit out
on heart and will and brain:
inspire your church with love and power
to ease our cities' pain!

O healing Savior, Prince of Peace,
salvation's source and sum,
for you our broken cities cry:
O come, Lord Jesus, come!
With truth your royal diadem,
with righteousness your rod,
O come, Lord Jesus, bring to earth
the city of our God!

Margaret Clarkson (b. 1915), 1981

Eucharist | Eschatology

Martha L. Moore-Keish

The 1984 movie *Places in the Heart* tells the story of Edna Spalding, a recently widowed white mother of two in a small Texas town during the Depression. Against all odds, with the help of a transient black man and a disagreeable blind boarder, she manages to plant and harvest her forty acres of cotton in order to keep her home. Around the edges of this central story, characters in the movie engage in murder, adultery, theft, assault, and plain old mean-spiritedness. The final scene shows a congregation in a local country church gathered to celebrate communion. As the cubes of bread and the tiny glasses of grape juice are passed down the pews, the camera focuses on one face after another: first, anonymous members of the community; then Edna's sister, who passes the tray to her cheating husband; then members of the Ku Klux Klan, who share the elements with the black man they had beaten up; then the Spalding children; then Edna herself; and finally Edna's husband, the town sheriff who had been shot and killed at the beginning of the film. Sheriff Spalding then quietly passes the bread and cup to the young black man who shot him with the words, "The peace of Christ."

What is going on here? Although the residents of Waxahachie, Texas, may not have used the words "Eucharist" and "eschatology," their actions in the final scene of the movie have much to teach us about the connection of these two theological terms. In that understated scene, the living and the dead, black and white, young and old, those who have sinned and those who have been sinned against, all sit together in the same dusty, whitewashed sanctuary to share the Lord's Supper. This is one picture of the joyful feast of God's people, in which they "will come from east and west, from north and south, and will eat in the kingdom of God" (Luke 13:29). Communion, from the earliest days of the church, has had something to do with hope for the future, with the consummation of all things, with "that great gettin' up morning." *Places in the Heart* gives us a glimpse of what that future might look like.

> Now Christ is the only food of our soul, and therefore our Heavenly Father invites us to Christ, that, refreshed by partaking of him, we may repeatedly gather strength until we shall have reached heavenly immortality.
>
> John Calvin

Many different terms are used for this Christian meal: Lord's Supper, Holy Communion, Eucharist, Mass. Each term has a particular history and emphasizes a particular dimension of the meal. "Lord's Supper," for instance, recalls the last meal Jesus shared with his disciples. This term tends to be used in traditions that focus on that meal as the precedent for what Christians do when they come to table today. "Eucharist" comes from the Greek word for "thanksgiving," and so the use of this term tends to emphasize the meal as an occasion for giving thanks to God for the gifts given in the sacrament. "Communion" focuses attention on the gathered community sharing the meal. "Mass" comes from the Latin phrase that dismisses the people at the conclusion of the service. It simply came to refer to the entire service. Though each term has its own context and set of associations, this essay will use a variety of terms interchangeably to refer to the meal, in recognition of the fact that the meal itself has many dimensions which cannot be expressed in a single name.

In some places, celebrations of communion, or the Eucharist, focus solely on the past. In such participations of the sacrament, we remember what Jesus Christ did with his disciples on that long-ago night when he was betrayed, and we repeat the same gestures to identify with the disciples. We recall the past in a way that makes the Supper look something like a funeral service for Jesus. Although communion always has an element of memory, in these instances the meal recalls only something that happened long ago.

In other places, the Eucharist is mainly a present-oriented event, focused on each individual's relationship with Jesus or on the transformation of the elements into the body of Christ. What seems to matter in these celebrations is the here and now, to the exclusion of both the historical tradition and the future hope. Although communion rightly includes attention to this time and this place, in these instances the meal focuses almost exclusively on the present moment.

Yet New Testament texts show us that the Supper also points ahead to a time when Christ will come again and all of creation will be made new. The Eucharist has to do with past and present, but it also has to do with the future — with eschatology. The doctrine of eschatology has sometimes been reduced to speculation about events in the distant (or not so distant) future. The "doctrine of last things" in some places has come to mean a listing of the particular events at the end of time, with the largest debates centering on when exactly Christ will return and what will happen at that point.

Eschatology is much more than mere speculation about the future. The eschatological character of Christian faith means that we have hope in the power of God over all that would hurt or destroy. We have confidence in God's ultimate purposes and goals for the restoration of creation. We have assurance that God will usher in the new heavens and the new earth, the place where the lion will lie down with the lamb and the child will play with the wild animals. Eschatology is not about idle speculation about who will be "left behind" at the rapture; it is about our hope in God. Furthermore, Christian eschatology affirms not only that we have hope that God will triumph over evil in some future time, but also that we participate already in that future. One way in which we participate in God's future now is by coming to the table to "proclaim the death of the Lord until he comes again."

Memory and Hope

From the earliest centuries of the church's history, when Christians have gathered to share the Lord's Supper, they have prayed before eating and drinking. These prayers, variously called Great Prayers of Thanksgiving, Eucharistic Prayers, Anaphoras, or Canons, have usually followed a Trinitarian pattern, beginning by praising God for the work of creation and salvation history, then remembering the life, death, and resurrection of Jesus Christ, and concluding with a section calling on the Holy Spirit to bless the elements in order that they may become the body and blood of Christ. This pattern makes it clear that the Eucharist is about both memory and hope.

The section of the prayer recounting the events of Jesus' life, death, and resurrection is called the anamnesis, or remembrance. One simple version of the anamnesis is as follows:

> Born of Mary, he shares our life.
> Eating with sinners, he welcomes us.
> Guiding his children, he leads us.
> Visiting the sick, he heals us.
> Dying on the cross, he saves us.
> Risen from the dead, he gives new life.
> Living with you, he prays for us.
> With thanksgiving we take this bread and this cup
> and proclaim the death and resurrection of our Lord.[1]

Clearly, the Eucharist is rooted in the memory of something that happened in the past. Gathered around a table, we remember the One who ate and drank with sinners and who broke bread with his disciples on the night of his arrest.

The Eucharist is also, however, about something that we anticipate. The prayer that tells the story of Jesus' actions two thousand years ago goes on to call on the Holy Spirit to sanctify this meal here and now and

---

1. Great Thanksgiving, in *Book of Common Worship*, Presbyterian Church (USA) (Louisville: Westminster/John Knox Press, 1993), p. 152.

turn us to the future, when we shall all sit at table together in the kingdom of God. This section is called the epiclesis (literally, "appeal or call"):

> Pour out your Holy Spirit upon us
> that this meal may be
> a communion in the body and blood of our Lord.
> Make us one with Christ
> and with all who share this feast.
> Unite us in faith,
> encourage us with hope,
> inspire us to love,
> that we may serve as your faithful disciples
> until we feast at your table in glory.[2]

The epiclesis forms a critical piece of the communion liturgy because it
calls on the Holy Spirit to make this meal and this gathered community
into the body of Christ for the world until he comes again. Looking back
at the pattern of God's work in the past, the prayer enables the church to
look to the future with hope.

Eucharist and eschatology, then, benefit from being considered together. The Eucharistic meal grows in significance when it regains its future dimension, and eschatology returns from obscurity when it is re-
connected with past events and present life. Both have everything to do
with who we are and how we live here and now.

The Already and the Not Yet

We commonly picture time as a line stretching from the shadowy past
to the shadowy future, with our present moment marked with vivid
clarity in the center of the diagram. History is linear, and we proceed
from one point in time to the next with all the certainty of an inch-
worm plotting its course along the edge of a leaf. Yet Christian eschatology and Eucharistic practice challenge this view of history. Since the

2. *Book of Common Worship*, p. 152.

revelation of God in Christ, we are caught up in God's future here and now; we are "tomorrow's people," to quote Reformed theologian Jean-Jacques von Allmen.[3] Each time we sit down together at the Lord's table, we remember the past, but we also recognize the presence of the Lord with us, and we anticipate the future time when Christ will be revealed in full glory to all the world. Past, present, and future are not mutually exclusive phases of history; the power of God's future animates our gatherings even today.

Geoffrey Wainwright helpfully describes two models of eschatology that have appeared in theological work of the past few decades: the vertical and the horizontal.[4] The horizontal is the more familiar to Western thinkers: eschatology refers to that future time when God will be all in all, when "all shall be well and all shall be well and all manner of thing shall be well," as Julian of Norwich once said. The future lies before us, and though we may eagerly lean into it, it is not here yet. In the Eucharist, worshipers acknowledge this form of eschatology when they "proclaim the death of the Lord *until he comes again*." According to the vertical model of eschatology, on the other hand, eternity breaks into human time "from above," as it were, at particular moments, such as the Incarnation, the Resurrection, and Eucharistic celebrations. All of time is enveloped in eternity, rather than eternity being simply the shadowy future that we anticipate. So, like the disciples on the road to Emmaus, when we break bread, we recognize the face of Christ across the table from us already. Each celebration of the Lord's Supper to some degree enacts the tension between these two eschatological models.

Calvin understood the vertical model of eschatology in a slightly different manner: eternity does not break in "from above"; rather, at the table of the Lord, we are lifted up by the Holy Spirit into the presence of Christ, seated at the right hand of God. For this reason, the words of the

3. Jean-Jacques von Allmen, *The Lord's Supper* (Richmond, Va.: John Knox Press, 1966), p. 106.

4. See Geoffrey Wainwright, *Eucharist and Eschatology*, 3rd ed. (Akron, Ohio: OSL Publications, 2002), pp. 14ff.

Sursum Corda — "Lift up your hearts"/"We lift them to the Lord" — have been central to the Reformed practice of Holy Communion. This dialogue reminds us that God does not come down to transform the elements but lifts us up to transform us into the body of Christ.

Another way of describing the two models of eschatology is to say that we live in a time when God's reign is both "already" (the vertical model) and "not yet" (the horizontal model). Jesus Christ has already introduced God's kingdom into the world, but it is not yet fully realized. Classical Eucharistic prayers hold these two eschatological models together: the Sanctus catches up the community in the "already" of the heavenly choir, singing "Holy, holy, holy Lord, God of power and might, heaven and earth are full of your glory," while the epiclesis usually has a reference to hope in the future time when "we will sit at table in Christ's kingdom."

For example, the epiclesis of the early Eucharistic prayer "The Anaphora of the Twelve Apostles" includes concern for both present and future life:

> We ask you therefore, almighty Lord and God of the holy powers, falling on our faces before you, that you send your Holy Spirit upon these offerings set before you, and show this bread to be the venerated body of our Lord Jesus Christ, that they may be to all who partake of them for life and resurrection, for forgiveness of sins, and health of soul and body, and enlightenment of mind, and defence before the dread judgement-seat of your Christ; and let no one of your people perish, Lord, but make us all worthy that, serving without disturbance and ministering before you at all times of our life, we may enjoy your heavenly and immortal and life-giving mysteries, through your grace and mercy and love for man, now (and to the ages of ages).[5]

This prayer suggests that those who partake of the holy meal receive "life and resurrection, . . . forgiveness of sins, . . . health of soul and body,

---

5. "The Anaphora of the Twelve Apostles," in *Prayers of the Eucharist: Early and Reformed*, ed. R. C. D. Jasper and G. J. Cuming, 3rd rev. ed. (Collegeville, Minn.: Liturgical Press, 1990), p. 127.

and enlightenment of mind" here and now, as firstfruits of the kingdom, but also that they may look forward to "defence before the dread judgement-seat of your Christ" at the end of time. Thus the Eucharist proclaims the presence of Christ even as it prays "Maranatha: Come, Lord Jesus." It directs worshipers' attention both to the now and to the ages of ages.

The Community and the Individual

Another feature that emerges when eschatology is considered in light of the Eucharist is that God's future includes people gathered in community, not individuals eating alone. In biblical accounts, meals are not individual but are by nature communal events. To "break bread" is to share food and drink with others, not to warm up something in the microwave and eat it alone in front of *Seinfeld* reruns. Many biblical writers present the picture of God's ultimate reign as that of a great feast at the end of time, when "many will come from east and west and will eat with Abraham and Isaac and Jacob in the kingdom of heaven" (Matt. 8:11). So from earliest days the community has been necessary for celebration of the Eucharistic meal, and the Eucharist has provided a foretaste of the eschatological feast of the Lamb (Rev. 19:9). The ancient Eucharistic prayer in the Didache says, "As this broken bread was scattered over the mountains, and when brought together became one, so let your church be brought together from the ends of the earth into your kingdom."[6] This petition reflects the church's understanding that through the action of the Holy Spirit, the

> [Jesus Christ] gave us a new birth in holy baptism and made us his own body, his own flesh, his offspring . . . and with a love like that of a natural mother he devised a way to feed us with his own body.
>
> Theodore of Mopsuestia

6. Didache, ch. 9, in *Prayers of the Eucharist: Early and Reformed*, p. 23.

bread broken and shared at the communion table draws people together into one and anticipates the time when all people will come together into God's universal reign.

The twentieth-century Scottish theologian Donald Baillie observed that one of the great gifts of the practice of communion in Reformed churches is the passing of the bread and wine down the pews, because this emphasizes the priesthood of all believers and the communal nature of the meal. This may not always be true in practice today — much of the time, pew communion can be an exercise in individual piety — but the impulse is right: this is a communal meal, not an individual snack.

The common practice of the Lord's Supper in Scottish churches following the Reformation points more clearly to the communal nature of the meal: on communion Sundays, members of the congregation literally gathered at tables that had been set in the sanctuary, sharing the bread and cup as they were passed. Some Scottish churches today preserve a remnant of this practice by covering the backs of the pews with "tablecloths," strips of white cloth secured with silver communion-cup holders, on communion Sundays. This reminds worshipers that they are gathered with others to celebrate a meal.

Coming forward to receive the bread and cup is another way of celebrating communion that enacts the corporate nature of the sacrament. A few years ago, a certain North American Presbyterian congregation with a long tradition of serving the people in the pews revised their practice out of necessity. During a lengthy renovation project, they worshiped between masses at the Roman Catholic church next door. Time and space constraints forced them to reconsider how they celebrated the sacrament. The worship leaders, without apology and without extensive explanation, decided to invite the congregation to come forward to receive the bread and cup. Suddenly, a meal that had encouraged people to focus inward turned into a corporate feast. People looked at one another. They smiled. Walking to the front of the sanctuary and then back to their seats, they became part of a grand procession of saints of all ages — and of all *the* ages.

As the feast of God's people here and now, the Eucharist reminds us that one day we will all sit at God's great "welcome table" and pass the food until all are filled. When the Holy Spirit enlivens our meals, we share in this abundant feast even now. Not only does this affirmation criticize any practice of communion that emphasizes individual experience over communal celebration, but it also criticizes any understanding of eschatology that focuses on individual salvation over the gathering of the whole church "from the ends of the earth into [God's] kingdom."

The Material and the Spiritual

Eschatology in light of the Eucharist involves the tension of the already and the not yet, and it emphasizes the community, not simply solitary individuals. A third theme that emerges when eschatology and Eucharist are considered together is that both of these embrace the material as well as the spiritual realm. The Eucharist clearly involves our bodies as well as our souls. This is God's gracious way of engaging our entire selves in encounter with Jesus Christ. Calvin affirmed this in his notion of accommodation. In both sacraments, said Calvin, God accommodates God's very self to our limitations: "Shut up as we are in the prison house of our flesh, we have not yet attained angelic rank. God, therefore, in his wonderful providence accommodating himself to our capacity, has prescribed a way for us, though still far off, to draw near to him."[7] One need not embrace Calvin's negative view of embodied humanity as a "prison house of flesh" to affirm with him that God's use of physical means to communicate with humanity is a gracious acknowledgment of our particular creaturely capacities. In the Lord's Supper, as also in baptism, God works through physical means to unite believers with Christ.

In the Eucharist, we are dealing with physical realities that involve our bodies; we are fed with loaf and cup. As Lawrence Stookey says, "To

---

7. John Calvin, *Institutes of the Christian Religion*, ed. John T. McNeill, trans. Ford Lewis Battles (Philadelphia: Westminster Press, 1960), 4.1.1.

remember (at the table) was to *do* something, not to think about something."[8] These symbols remind us that Jesus Christ was incarnate, that he too needed food and drink. And they remind us that we as human beings require food and drink. Symbols like these communicate with our embodied selves in a way that words alone cannot do.

Just as the Lord's Supper involves our bodies as well as the less tangible dimensions of our selves, so also eschatology has implications for the material as well as the spiritual realm. One way of talking about this is in the language of the Apostles' Creed, which affirms the "resurrection of the body." As Jesus proclaims in the Gospel of John, "Those who eat my flesh and drink my blood have eternal life, and I will raise them up on the last day" (John 6:54). Whatever this may mean, it surely affirms that God's future involves our embodied selves and not just some ethereal essence detached from material reality. In the last days, according to various biblical descriptions, there will be eating, drinking, singing, and the joy of seeing the Lord face to face. If we are to trust such accounts, then at the end of time, God will not simply abandon these flesh-and-blood creations formed out of dust, and even these squishy, bony, vulnerable bodies, which give us so much pain and so much delight, will dance again at the wedding feast of the Lamb.

When we come together at the Lord's table now, our bodies both anticipate and enact God's future reign. As John's Gospel puts it, at the table we receive Christ's body and blood, which nourishes us on eternal life and prepares us for the future. At the same time, we become members of Christ's body so that even now we live out God's intention for the world. This means that our participation in the Lord's Supper places ethical claims on our lives. For example, as Gordon Lathrop puts it, the "economy of the eucharist" is in critical dialogue with all other means of distributing food.[9] Because our bodies are living out God's future today, we cannot ignore the injustices and abuses of this world. As those who

8. Lawrence Stookey, *Eucharist: Christ's Feast with the Church* (Nashville: Abingdon Press, 1993), p. 28.

9. Gordon Lathrop, *Holy People: A Liturgical Ecclesiology* (Minneapolis: Fortress Press, 1999), p. 165.

are fed on kingdom food, we are claimed in body, mind, and soul to witness to the coming reign of God.

In his book *Torture and Eucharist*, William Cavanaugh tells of the change in Roman Catholic Eucharistic practice in Chile during the Pinochet regime, a change that embraced the material implications of the sacrament. At the beginning of those years, the consensus among Chilean Catholic leaders was that the church was responsible for people's souls, while the state was responsible for their bodies. This left the church with few resources to address the horrific cases of torture perpetrated by the nation's military leaders. As the years passed and the numbers of the "disappeared" grew, however, leaders in the church came to realize that they did bear responsibility for the treatment of people's bodies — that to be the body of Christ meant to care for the bodies of the broken. They began to recognize that the Eucharist establishes an alternative body to the body of the state, and indeed that true participation in the Eucharist requires Christians to go out and witness to God's vision of life, forgiveness, and health for all the world. Through renewed attention to its Eucharistic practices, then, the church became a lively community that spoke out against the torture of the state, contributing to the eventual downfall of Pinochet.[10]

In North America, Eucharistic practices that emphasize the abundance of God's goodness to us should provoke participants to wonder about those who do not have enough to eat, who are not recipients of such abundance. One congregation, in reflecting on this, has revived a Eucharistic practice of the ancient church: members of the congregation bring many loaves of bread to church on communion Sundays, and of those many loaves, one is shared by the congregation at communion. The rest of the loaves are taken after worship and distributed to the hungry of the community through a nearby food pantry. In this way, members of the congregation are living out their role as participants in the reign of God here and now, feeding the hungry in the expectation of the day "when all will sit at table in the kingdom of God."

10. William Cavanaugh, *Torture and Eucharist: Theology, Politics, and the Body of Christ* (Oxford: Blackwell Publishers, 1998).

Judgment and Renewal

Both eschatology and the Lord's Supper include moments of judgment and renewal. It is difficult to talk about judgment in relation to the Lord's Supper in this time; after all, we do not want to repeat the fearful assertions of our ancestors that no one should come to the table except those who are somehow worthy and understand fully what they are doing. Nevertheless, we cannot ignore the passages from 1 Corinthians that state, "You cannot drink the cup of the Lord and the cup of demons. You cannot partake of the table of the Lord and the table of demons" (1 Cor. 10:21), and "Whoever, therefore, eats the bread or drinks the cup of the Lord in an unworthy manner will be answerable for the body and blood of the Lord. . . . For all who eat and drink without discerning the body, eat and drink judgment against themselves" (1 Cor. 11:27, 29). Nor can we ignore the Gospels' references to a final judgment that will exclude some from the banquet. As Matthew has it, "Many will come from east and west and will eat with Abraham and Isaac and Jacob in the kingdom of heaven, while the heirs of the kingdom will be thrown into the outer darkness, where there will be weeping and gnashing of teeth" (Matt. 8:11-12).

The Supper is not, then, simply sweetness and light; it is also an anticipation of the Last Judgment. To use the language of the World Council of Churches Assembly at Canberra in 1991, communion is a gracious *gift*, but it is also a *call* to faithful living.[11] If we do not heed that call, we are subject to judgment. This image of judgment may be chilling to those of us who hear the plaintive cries at the end of Matthew 25: "Lord, when was it that we saw you hungry or thirsty or a stranger or naked or sick or in prison and did not take care of you?" Yet God's final judgment is not first and foremost about casting people into outer darkness. Rather, this judgment is good news for two reasons.

First, God in Christ cares about the "least of these." We may cringe at

---

11. "Baptism and the Unity of the Church: A Study Paper" by the Institute for Ecumenical Research, in *Baptism and the Unity of the Church*, ed. Michael Root and Risto Saarinen (Grand Rapids: Eerdmans/WCC, 1998), p. 19.

the image of some being cast into eternal fire, but the point is that Jesus Christ has special concern for the powerless and how they are treated. Our actions count for something. This does not mean that we can earn salvation, but it does mean that the smallest kindness, even if ignored by society, is noticed by Christ. More than this, the smallest kindness, even if ignored by society, is *done for* Christ. Better to live in this kind of cosmos than to dwell in a world where cruelty and kindness have the same ultimate reward.

Second, judgment is good news because the Judge is also the Redeemer. The One who sits on the throne also came to rescue us from our sins. As Calvin says, "No mean assurance, this — that we shall be brought before no other judgment seat than that of our Redeemer, to whom we must look for our salvation!"[12] This is good news, for we are not necessarily among the righteous. We walk by the hungry on our way to buy groceries. We drive past those shivering in the cold on our way home from work. If the final judgment were all we knew of Christ, we would be doomed. But this Judge, this King of the poor and hungry, reaches right down even to us, to heal us of our self-importance, to rescue us from our narrow view of the world, to turn us around and offer us new life. This Judge shows us that we, even we, are among the least of these whom Christ came to save.

Thanks be to God that the day of judgment is also the day of renewal. Thanks be that the Judge is also the Redeemer. Thanks be that even the *Dies Irae*, the ominous portion of the funeral mass that evokes the coming of Christ in final judgment, also recognizes that the One who brings judgment is the One who grants us peace.[13] The final days, according to Christian vision, are good news of God's final triumph over evil and death. For this reason, the earliest Christians looked forward to

12. Calvin, *Institutes*, 2.16.18.

13. The *Dies Irae* begins *Dies irae, dies illa, solvet saeculum in favilla, teste David cum Sibylla* ("That day of wrath, that dreadful day, shall heaven and earth in ashes lay, as David and the Sybil say"), but it ends *Pie Iesu Domine, dona eis requiem. Amen.* ("Lord, have mercy, Jesus blest, grant them all Your Light and Rest. Amen."). The Latin is from *Roman Breviary*, the translation from the 1962 Missal, which is partially based upon the work of Father James Ambrose Dominic Aylward (1813-1872) and William F. Wingfield (1813-1874).

the final judgment not with fear, apparently, but with joy. Centuries later, Hans Schwarz tells us, "Martin Luther recaptured this New Testament confidence in the face of the judgment when, contrary to the mood of the Middle Ages, he did not conceive of this as a day of wrath, but as a day of the glory of God, a day to which he was looking forward when he said in many of his letters: 'Come, dear, last day.'"[14]

So also the Supper, even as it presents a moment of judgment, also (and primarily) presents us with new life and forgiveness of sin. We need not avoid the Eucharist, as many did in centuries past, for fear of judgment. Rather, we need to approach the table with eagerness; as hymnwriter Brian Wren puts it, "I come with joy, a child of God, forgiven, loved, and free,/the life of Jesus to recall, in love laid down for me."[15]

It is also crucial to remember that judgment lies not only ahead of us. In Christ's death and resurrection, judgment and redemption have

---

Walk together, children, don't you get weary . . .
there's a great camp meeting in the promised land.

African American Heritage Hymnal, no. 541

---

already occurred. In the words "This is my body, broken for you," we recall that Jesus has already assumed our sins and suffered the judgment that humanity could not suffer. The Heidelberg Catechism asks in words strange to contemporary ears, "What comfort does the return of Christ 'to judge the living and the dead' give you?" and the response is this: "That in all affliction and persecution I may await with head held high the very Judge from heaven *who has already* submitted himself to the judgment of God for me and has removed all the curse from me."[16] Just as we

---

14. Hans Schwarz, *Eschatology* (Grand Rapids: Eerdmans, 2000), p. 392.

15. Brian Wren, "I Come with Joy," *The Covenant Hymnal: A Worshipbook,* no. 550 (Chicago: Covenant Publications, 1996).

16. Heidelberg Catechism, Question 52, emphasis mine.

live in the "already" and the "not yet" of God's reign, so also we live in the "already" and "not yet" of final judgment.

At the table, we recognize the seriousness of our actions; we are called to "discern the body" of Christ in the gathered community around us, and not to approach the Supper carelessly. If we participate in the Eucharist and then walk out of the church and oppress our neighbor, then surely we do open ourselves to God's judgment, for we have not allowed ourselves to be changed by the encounter with the living Christ. Yet the table first and foremost offers us forgiveness for all of our wrongdoings and an opportunity to eat and drink the feast of the new creation. As "The Anaphora of the Twelve Apostles" puts it, at the table we pray "that [the bread and cup] may be to all who partake of them for life and resurrection, for forgiveness of sins, and health of soul and body, and enlightenment of mind, and defence before the dread judgement-seat of your Christ." Here at the table we receive both judgment and renewal, even as we look ahead to God's renewing judgment on that "dear, last day."

Universality of Vision

The final scene of *Places in the Heart* shows all the members of the Waxahachie community — rich and poor, black and white, those who have sinned blatantly and those who have been sinned against — all gathered together at the Lord's Supper. This unlikely gathering shows a final characteristic of the Eucharistic meal, one that also characterizes the Christian eschatological vision: namely, the table, like God's kingdom, welcomes people from all the corners of the world. In Luke's Gospel, Jesus tells his disciples that "people will come from east and west, from north and south, and will eat in the kingdom of God" (Luke 13:29). Jesus said this in reference to the last days, but significantly, these words have become a common part of the invitation to communion. This meal shows us what it means to sit down in the kingdom of God: that those whom we least expect to meet will smile at us from across the table, passing the bread and murmuring, "The peace of Christ."

Many rural churches in North Carolina have a tradition called "ingathering," a custom growing out of the celebration of the abundant harvest in autumn. An ingathering is usually an occasion for the production of huge quantities of barbecue of the pulled-pork variety native to that state. People stream in from city and country, both strangers and friends, young and old, to sit at table and feast on this luscious dish that has been cooking slowly for at least twenty-four hours. At such an event, "ingathering" refers both to the harvest and to the people who are so gathered. This, too, is a portrait of the eschatological meal: those in overalls and those sweating in business suits sit side by side, licking their fingers in delight before laden paper plates and plastic utensils at God's great banquet.

Nor does the eschatological vision concern people alone. At the end of time, according to Revelation, heaven and earth as we know them will pass away, and there will be a new heaven and a new earth. All of creation will be remade — but a creation without death, without night, a place where "mourning and crying and pain will be no more" (Rev. 21:4) because the glory of the Lord will be all in all.

The Russian Orthodox theologian Alexander Schmemann understands all of creation in sacramental terms. Although the world is fallen, longing for healing and transformation in a new heaven and new earth, the sacraments reveal the goodness of God's creation and the hope for God's re-creation. He says,

> If in baptism, water can become a "laver of regeneration," if our earthly food — bread and wine — can be transformed into partaking of the body and blood of Christ, if with oil we are granted the anointment of the Holy Spirit, if, to put it briefly, everything in the world can be identified, manifested, and understood as a gift of God and participation in the new life, it is because all of creation was originally summoned and destined for the fulfillment of the divine economy — "then God will be all in all."[17]

Creation, too, is implicated in our sacramental participation, because when we encounter the presence of Christ in the bread and cup,

17. Alexander Schmemann, *The Eucharist: Sacrament of the Kingdom* (Crestwood, N.Y.: St. Vladimir's Seminary Press, 1988), pp. 33-34.

we witness to the possibility that not just these gifts but all of God's created order will one day bear the presence of the divine.

Not just people but animals too will share food in those last days, according to Isaiah — and the animal table partners will be as odd as the human ones:

> The wolf shall live with the lamb,
> the leopard shall lie down with the kid,
> the calf and the lion and the fatling together,
> and a little child shall lead them.
> The cow and the bear shall graze,
> their young shall lie down together;
> and the lion shall eat straw like the ox.
> The nursing child shall play over the hole of the asp,
> and the weaned child shall put its hand on the adder's den.
> They will not hurt or destroy on all my holy mountain;
> for the earth will be full of the knowledge of the LORD
> as the waters cover the sea. (Isa. 11:6-9)

What does it mean to eat in the kingdom of God? For people, it will mean encountering those we never expected to meet across the table from us. For animals, it will mean changing eating habits so much that what used to be dinner is now a dinner companion. For all creation, it means utter transformation into God's original purpose: manifesting the glory of God.

Can we imagine what this might look like? In this life, in this perpetual tension between Good Friday and Easter morning, we can only catch glimpses of such glory. Yet now and then, in Waxahachie, Texas, or on the West Bank, in Northern Ireland or North Korea, when enemies break bread together or when the veil between the living and the dead momentarily lifts, then God's future breaks in, and we hear in the distance, "Hallelujah! For the Lord our God the Almighty reigns. Let us rejoice and exult and give him the glory, for the marriage of the Lamb has come" (Rev. 19:6b-7a).

The Offering

Many North American Protestant churches include as a regular part of worship something called "the offering," which usually refers to the gathering of money from people seated in the pews and the ritual procession of that money to the front of the church during the singing of the Doxology to the tune of "Old Hundredth." What many worshipers may not realize is that this "offering" is a remnant of the ancient practice of bringing forward the gifts of bread and wine at communion, an offering which at some times and places also included the bringing forward of monetary gifts. In the classic pattern of the early church, the offertory constituted the first movement of the Eucharist: the bringing of the gifts to the table so that they might be offered to the people as "the gifts of God for the people of God."

During the course of the medieval period, however, laypeople participated in communion less and less frequently. The Eucharist became primarily a spectacle, a visual event to witness from afar, as the priest raised the host and the bell was rung to signify the transformation of the bread into the body of Christ. Priests and members of religious orders might commune as much as every day, but the vast majority of Christians declined to commune for fear of doing so unworthily. Many received communion only once a year, at the most.

Meanwhile, the offertory procession continued, but it became less about preparing the table for the meal and more about presenting monetary gifts. The monetary gifts themselves, which in earlier centuries had included alms for the poor, became primarily a way to fund the services of the church.

The sixteenth-century reformers had many complaints about the medieval Roman Catholic sacramental practices, including the elaborate pomp and ceremony that they judged to detract from the central matters of Word and Sacrament. The grand offertory processions were among the practices eliminated by the reformers, although Zwingli and Calvin both retained the simple practice of bringing bread and wine to the table immediately before communion. Many Reformation churches, including Strasbourg, Augsburg, and Basel, returned to the ancient practice of keeping a collection box outside the door of the sanctuary, so that people could place their monetary offerings there as they entered or left worship.[18] This removed the ostentatious parade of monetary gifts from the center of the service and kept the offertory procession for its original use: preparing for the Eucharistic feast.

In the context of the Eucharist, the offering can be a powerful enactment of the eschatological vision. This kind of procession, which offers to God "the fruit of our lands and the work of our hands"[19] in response to God's abundant goodness, can point toward the great procession of the nations into the new Jerusalem in the last days: "The nations will walk by its light, and the kings of the earth will bring their glory into it. . . . People will bring into it the glory and the honor of the nations" (Rev. 21:24, 26). When money is carried forward behind the primary gifts of the bread and cup, it is clear that what we are celebrating is not our own generosity but God's generosity to us.

"We give thee but thine own,/whate'er the gift may be" goes the old hymn, and this attitude appropriately characterizes any sort of offering, monetary or otherwise, in a worship service. "All that we have is thine alone/A trust, O Lord, from thee."[20] This is the point made by Paul when he says to the church in Corinth, "For all things are yours, whether Paul or Apollos or Cephas or the world or life or death or the present or the future — all belong to you, and you belong to Christ, and Christ belongs to God" (1 Cor. 3:21b-23). In the new creation, in which we live already and for which we await with eager longing, all things are ours to give because all things belong to God.

A similar sentiment was expressed by John Wesley in his sermon "The Use of Money":

18. For much of the preceding history, see Brant Copeland, "A Modest Proposal: Get Rid of the Offering," in *Call to Worship: Liturgy, Music, Preaching, and the Arts* 35, no. 4 (2002): 5-13.

19. Michael Joncas, "We Come to Your Feast," in *Gather Comprehensive*, no. 850 (Chicago: GIA Publications, Inc., 1994).

20. William Walsham How, "We Give Thee But Thine Own" (1858), in *The Hymnbook* (Richmond, Va.: Presbyterian Church in the United States, 1955), no. 312.

Render unto God not a tenth, not a third, not half, but all that is God's (be it more or less) by employing all on yourself, your household, the household of faith and all mankind, in such a manner that you may give a good account of your stewardship when ye can be no longer stewards; in such a manner as the oracles of God direct, both by general and particular precepts; in such a manner that, whatever ye do may be "a sacrifice of a sweet-smelling savour to God" [cf. Lev. 8:21], and that every act may be rewarded in that day when the Lord cometh with all his saints.[21]

We give because God first gave to us. We give because everything that we have belongs to the gracious Giver of all things. We give because we live already in the heavenly city, in which God is all in all. If our act of offering in worship embodies this attitude, however imperfectly, then God will be glorified.

The Table of Tomorrow's People

During my first year of seminary, our community celebrated one particularly memorable communion service which, like the final scene of *Places in the Heart,* anticipated God's great "welcome table." A few hundred of us were gathered in a lecture hall, sharing the Lord's Supper at the conclusion of a lecture series on campus. The worship planners had listed in the bulletin a few hymns for us to sing while the bread and cup were being distributed. When we reached the end of the list, however, the elements were still being passed down the pews. In the midst of the awkward silence, a single voice, then a few voices, and soon the whole congregation began to sing "Let Us Break Bread Together":

Let us break bread together on our knees,
Let us break bread together on our knees,

21. John Wesley, "The Use of Money," in *John Wesley,* ed. Albert C. Outler (New York: Oxford University Press, 1964), pp. 249-50. Masculine references to humanity have not been changed from the original.

When I fall on my knees, with my face to the rising sun,
O Lord, have mercy on me.

What was going on here? A cynic might say that this was an example of a bunch of nervous and overly pious seminary students who had to fill up the unplanned space with something rather than sit in silence. Viewed in another way, however, this was a celebration of God's eschatological reign. "Let us break bread together" — is this a reference to the breaking of bread here and now, or is it a yearning for the time when we will all break bread together with Abraham, Isaac, and Jacob at God's great banquet table? Is this the "already" or the "not yet"? What about "When I fall on my knees" — is this present or future tense? I think the answer is "yes." Each of us individually and all of us together joined to affirm that here and now and in the time to come we will fall on our knees before the glory of God. On paper, "with my face to the rising sun" is clearly a reference to the natural wonder of a sunrise, but when sung, it also celebrates the resurrection of the risen Son of God. "O Lord, have mercy on me," we concluded, offering a prayer in the face of the coming judgment as well as a recognition of the redeeming love of God.

Whenever Christians break bread together on their knees, they are also summoned to turn their faces to the rising sun/Son. At these moments, they recognize in their midst and on the horizon the One who was and is and is to come. At these moments, the Eucharistic meal truly becomes a foretaste of the glory divine.

> Hope arises out of the hard truth of how things are. Christians will always live carrying in one hand the promises of how it will be and in the other hand the hard reality of how it is. To deny either is to hold only half the truth of the gospel.
>
> Craig Barnes

Remembering with Love and Hope

Remembering with love and hope,
we celebrate the feast.
Christ bids us come and dine with him,
our Host and great High Priest.

God's Word made known in flesh and blood,
a covenant of grace;
in manger, cross, and empty tomb,
we see God's loving face.

Through all our lives, Lord, you are near,
and to the end of time.
In bread and cup yourself you give;
our life in yours we find.

We break the bread and bless the cup;
your Spirit is outpoured.
Made one in you, we feast in love
until you come, O Lord.

We trust this pledge of your strong love
and pray, your kingdom come,
when face to face we'll feast with you
in our eternal home.

John Paarlberg (b. 1950)

I Come with Joy, a Child of God

I come with joy, a child of God,
forgiven, loved, and free,
the life of Jesus to recall,
in love laid down for me.

I come with Christians far and near
to find, as all are fed,
the new community of love
in Christ's communion bread.

As Christ breaks bread and bids us share,
each proud division ends.
The love that made us, makes us one,
and strangers now are friends.

The Spirit of the risen Christ,
unseen, but ever near,
is in such friendship better known,
alive among us here.

Together met, together bound
by all that God has done,
we'll go with joy, to give the world
the love that makes us one.

Brian Wren

Ending of Worship | Ethics

David L. Stubbs

"When will this service end?" When I was a child, that was the question that tugged at my mind during worship at our family's local Lutheran church. I could hardly wait for the end of the service so that I could change out of my uncomfortable church clothes, get outdoors, and start playing. Even though I liked many things about church, the Sunday services still seemed a bit long. The idea of heaven being an eternal Sunday worship service — while I knew I should somehow be happy about that prospect — was cold comfort for me. Perhaps the services would be better in heaven, but for now, worship seemed to get in the way of my life as a kid.

In high school, my question "When will this service end?" expanded to include an impatience not only with particular Sunday worship hours but also with what I called "liturgical" worship as a whole. I had begun going with some friends to larger, nondenominational churches that were also "non-liturgical." While this term makes little sense — for there was, of course, a form and hence a "liturgy" in those so-called non-liturgical services — the term does point to something substantial: namely, contemporary forms and music, extemporaneous prayer, and an overall "looser" feel. In those worship experiences, I discovered a newfound joy and sense of closeness to God. I also felt that those worship experiences were in some way more connected to the rest of my life as a whole. At least the music seemed "relevant." As a result, I developed an allergy to "liturgy," which for me meant "old" and thus "dead" forms, music, and words. My question thus changed to "When will this 'liturgy' end?"

Looking back, I do not think it was the liturgy or lack of liturgy per se that was important to me. I wanted an end to disconnection. What I wanted was a greater sense of connection to God and a sense that my worship was linked to the rest of my life. I felt a greater sense of those connections in the more contemporary forms. It felt authentic, real.

> In worship we receive the self-giving love of God, and the test of our thankfulness is whether we reproduce that pattern of self-giving in our daily relationships with other people. Of course, the test already begins with our attitudes and behavior as brothers and sisters in the liturgical assembly.
>
> Geoffrey Wainwright

The connection (or disconnection) of our worship to life is often reflected in another "end" of the service, "end" now meaning the final moments or actions of the service. While the ending moments of a worship service are brief, they are, like all endings and partings, filled with meaning. We tend to place a lot of interpretive weight on endings. "All's well that ends well," we say. Such moments of ending are opportunities to reflect on what has happened and what comes next. They help us sum up and understand all that has gone before and direct our thinking about what comes after. Thus, the ending of our worship services or liturgies can help us see if and how our worship is connected to the rest of our lives.

In the contemporary services I was part of, after the usually upbeat final chorus, the leader would say something like, "Have a great week, see you next time, and bring a friend!" That informal way of concluding seemed much more "real" to me than the service ending of my home church. In that more traditional setting, the service often ended with a grand organ postlude performance. People were informally encouraged to stay and listen and often clapped following the postlude. While I enjoyed the music, my experience of the service was that much of the worship was centered on the music and the "performers."

While I initially judged the contemporary services in general to be more "real" and "connected," I am no longer so sure of that. Worship of any kind of flavor, from anywhere on the spectrum of what is often referred to as "contemporary" or "traditional," or from any variety of types or cultural backgrounds can be seen as a self-contained whole with only limited connection to the rest of our life. All too often, instead of our worship service being "the point of concentration at which the whole of the Christian life comes to ritual focus," our worship remains fragmented from the rest of our lives.[1] The "see you next week" ending does not suggest that the activities performed in the service will somehow be embodied in the rest of our lives. Instead, it could be the ending of any meeting, from the local parent-teacher organization, to the foreign film club, to the tai chi class. The contemporary worship service was about praising God and being filled with a joy and an experience that would last until the next meeting. It did not necessarily inform me what the rest of my life was about. Similarly, the ending of the "traditional" service did not suggest much continuity with the rest of life. My experience of it was that it ended like most other performances. The ending did not suggest any ways that the worship experience might be connected ethically, morally, or even "spiritually" with the rest of life.

Endings and Final Ends

Certainly the renewed connection with God that took place during those services — which I believe was the primary goal of both the traditional and the contemporary services I was part of — was assumed by the pastors and worship leaders to have ramifications for all of life. The general principle might be that all of life is to be lived in general and undefined "gratitude" for the "grace" we receive in the worship service. While that is certainly true, Christian worship and liturgy can and should function in ways that are both deeper and more explicit. While

1. Geoffrey Wainwright, *Doxology: The Praise of God in Worship, Doctrine, and Life* (New York: Oxford University Press, 1980), p. 8.

there are many things that happen in worship, one function the liturgy — here understood as the total experience of corporate Christian worship when it follows the basic traditional elements of worship — has been understood to play is that it provides a window into the "final ends" or overarching purposes of human life as intended by God. Worship, in short, re-enacts or dramatizes God's intent for human flourishing. Worship gives us an opportunity to "practice" patterns of eternity.

This function of our corporate worship may be quite foreign to people in our churches today. I imagine that many people, in talking about going to church on Sundays, would say that their "worship experience" gives them a nice break from their busy week. After their pleasant experience, in which they might have learned something about God and were hopefully energized in some way, they are now ready to get back to their "regular" activities in "the real world." But by using the phrase "the real world" to speak of that portion of their life outside of worship, they are implying that what happens on Sunday mornings either is "un-real" or has a different sort of "spiritual reality" with little connection to their "public reality."

The origins of the word "liturgy" point us in quite a different direction. The term "liturgy" was originally rooted in the context of ancient Greek life, where it meant "the work of the people" and referred to "public works" such as the building of a bridge or the sponsorship of public entertainment.[2] Thus the word seems to indicate that the liturgy of the Christian worship service *is* the actions and work of the people. We, of course, use it most commonly to refer to the *blueprints* for that work rather than to the work itself. The liturgy, for us, is the printed order of worship. The Eastern Orthodox have a phrase that retains the earlier meaning of the word: "the liturgy after the Liturgy." This refers to the weeklong liturgy of our daily work done after the weekly Liturgy of our corporate worship. This phrase also implies that the work we do on Sundays in corporate worship is not somehow "unreal" but rather the "most real" work that we do.

2. Rodney Clapp, *A Peculiar People: The Church as Culture in a Post-Christian Society* (Downers Grove, Ill.: InterVarsity Press, 1996), p. 80.

By saying that corporate worship is the "most real" part of our week, I mean that in it we are in touch in an intense and powerful way with the patterns of the kingdom of God. The actions we perform and the way our minds, language, and emotions are formed in our performance of the liturgy are at the heart of our lives as Christians. In the liturgy, in our worship, we are not simply being presented with information, much less simply being entertained; rather, we are being made into Christians — our actions and lives are being linked to the life of the world, our hearts to the heart of God, our minds to the Truth. The liturgy is the embodiment of the patterns of the kingdom of God in summary fashion.[3] Liturgy thus might be described as a "window" of the kingdom. Or, put slightly differently, we might say that in the liturgy our actions — our prayers, praise, confession, offering, passing of the peace of Christ, openness to the Word of God — become transparent to the patterns of the kingdom. In those typical patterns, actions, and words, we encounter God and find our "real life," our "final ends," our ultimate goals. Just as the ending of the liturgy might recap and provide meaning to the whole service, liturgy as a whole can be seen as relating to the whole of life as its "end" or goal.

> In worship we practice the basic skills of our faith. We practice them over and over again so that they become second nature to us, and in becoming second nature, they become the way we see the world and live in it.
>
> Anthony B. Robinson

3. Stanley Hauerwas uses the idea of liturgy as "summary" in "The Liturgical Shape of the Christian Life: Teaching Christian Ethics as Worship," unpublished paper, pp. 14-15. Reinhard Hütter argues that theology, understood as a church practice, is a specific kind of "unfolding" of "God's economy of salvation," in *Suffering Divine Things: Theology as Church Practice* (Grand Rapids: Eerdmans, 2000), p. 180. The description of liturgy as a "window" is linked to the theology of icons. See Leonid Ouspensky and Vladimir Lossky, *The Meaning of Icons* (Crestwood, N.Y.: St. Vladimir's Seminary Press, 1989).

The Liturgy after the Liturgy: Liturgy and Ethics

However, we often reverse this relationship. Rather than allowing worship to enfold us in larger patterns of God's activity, we want worship to somehow equip us for what we consider "real life." Worship equips us to live our lives more joyfully, kindly, and energetically. But to determine *what* we should do, what purposes we should pursue and specific actions we should take in those pursuits, our "ethics," we take our cues from elsewhere. For example, if you think back to the latest newspaper article you read that dealt with an ethical issue, or to that undergraduate ethics class you took in college, I would doubt that the class or the article even mentioned Christian worship or liturgy. And conversely, when Christian people think about Sunday worship, I doubt many consider it a highly charged ethical activity. I know I at least did not have that understanding when I was growing up in our church. However, our corporate worship life as Christians does have great potential to shape and inform our ethical thinking — and in fact does so, whether or not we are aware of it.

But to see why this might be the case, we should define our terms more carefully. What is ethics? In Karl Barth's discussions of ethics in the *Church Dogmatics*, he says that ethics most generally is an attempt to define the standard or law or value by which we can judge human action. It is an attempt to come up with a standard by which we can call something good or evil. That is the first task of ethics.

Barth quite insightfully links the attempt to answer this question with the Fall. He writes,

> For man is not content simply to be the answer to [the ethical] question by the grace of God. He wants to be like God. He wants to know of himself (as God does) what is good and evil. He therefore wants to give this answer himself and of himself. So, then, as a result and in prolongation of the fall, we have "ethics," or, rather, the multifarious ethical systems, the attempted human answers to the ethical question.[4]

4. Karl Barth, *Church Dogmatics* (Edinburgh: T&T Clark, 1957), II.2, p. 517.

Instead of asking *this* question on good and evil, Barth claims that the first task of *Christian* ethics is to simply point to the covenant that God has established with humankind. Obedience to that covenant, that command, *is* the human good. Thus Christian ethics is a description of sanctified human life. Put another way, the task of Christian ethics is to describe the shape of the kingdom of God.

How then do we know that shape? Does the kingdom of God function according to certain laws, like most human kingdoms? If so, where is this command found, and what is its content? For Barth, Jesus Christ is the Command of God. What he means by this is that Jesus Christ is the image of God, and this image is the standard we are called to. Being conformed to the image of God is the goal of sanctification and the Command that human life is called to obey.

For Barth, the image of God is not some faculty, some "thing" that God possesses and has also given to humans, but rather a triune *pattern of activity*. Barth writes, "And this obedience of Jesus is the clear reflection of the unity of the Father and the Son by the bond of the Spirit in the being of the eternal God Himself, who is the fullness of all freedom."[5] This eternal obedience of the Son to the Father in the Spirit is incarnated in Jesus Christ; therefore, this pattern of activity is not a principle or a rule, but rather a Way. Christian ethics, in being a description of the Command of God for human life, is confronted not with a rule, or set of rules, but, as Barth says, by "the reality fulfilled in the person of Jesus Christ. This person as such is not only the ground and content but also the form of the divine command."[6]

Barth's description of a proper Christian ethics has much in common with the historical Christian tradition, for the Greek Fathers had a saying that Jesus was the *autobasilea*, the "Kingdom in himself."[7] Christian ethics must be theologically informed, meaning that insofar as ethics is a description of the good human life, the only way for us to "do eth-

5. Barth, *Church Dogmatics* II.2, p. 605.
6. Barth, *Church Dogmatics* II.2, p. 606.
7. Origen, "Commentary on Matthew," in *Ante-Nicene Fathers* (New York: Scribner's, 1926), p. 498.

ics" is to reflect on the patterns of activity that God has planned for us humans in his kingdom.

So, how do liturgy and ethics intersect? Put most simply: Christian ethics is a description of the kingdom of God, which is itself seen most clearly in the patterns of activity enfleshed in Jesus Christ. In the patterns of the liturgy we come into contact with those patterns of Christ. Because of this, as we are formed through a habitual participation in the liturgy, we grow in our ability to see the world and act in the world as Christians.

> When worship occurs, people are characterized, given their life and their fundamental location and orientation in the world.
>
> Don Saliers

This emphasis on the way that our liturgical practices inform our ethics is reflected in the work of three quite different twentieth-century theologians: Karl Barth, a part of the Reformed tradition; John Howard Yoder, an Anabaptist theologian; and Alexander Schmemann, a Russian Orthodox theologian.

It is instructive to note that Barth's ethics of reconciliation, when completed, was to have revolved around three central pieces of liturgy: baptism, the Lord's Prayer, and the Lord's Supper. John Webster, a trustworthy interpreter of Barth, writes that Barth's entire dogmatics is "an extended inquiry into the moral field — into the space within which moral agents act, and into the shape of their action, a shape given above all by the fact that their acts take place in the history of encounter between God as prime agent and themselves as those called to act in correspondence to the grace of God."[8] Seeing that Barth's ethics do revolve around this idea of human correspondence to and in the context of the grace of God, it is especially interesting to note Barth's high regard for the liturgical actions of baptism, prayer, and the Lord's Supper. Barth calls these liturgical actions of human response "kingdom-like" — Barth's highest compliment. For example, Barth says that all of human

---

8. John Webster, *Barth's Ethics of Reconciliation* (Cambridge: Cambridge University Press, 1995), p. 4.

life is to be the "dynamic actualization" of the Lord's Prayer: "He [God] wills that their whole life become invocation of this kind."⁹ Sanctified human activity is "summarized" in at least these three liturgical actions, actions that also serve to frame the "moral field." Prayer and the sacraments, for Barth, shape and frame Christian moral activity because they are unique in their ability to correspond to the grace of God.

In his intriguing and suggestive book entitled *Body Politics: Five Practices of the Christian Community Before the Watching World,* John Howard Yoder discusses what he calls five "liturgical" practices: baptism, Eucharist, mutual correction, the diversification of gifts and ministry, and open dialogue under the direction of the Holy Spirit.¹⁰ He claims these practices both form the "real world" for Christians and function as "paradigms" for all our action. He gets these practices from his study of the New Testament, showing that Jesus commanded them and tracing their precedents back into the liturgical life of Israel.¹¹ Using sacramental language to describe them, he further writes, "They are actions of God, in and with, through and under what men and women do. Where they are happening, the people of God is real in the world."¹² He ends his book with these intriguing comments: "It should not be surprising if there were such a deep structure that, once discerned in the five places where we have touched it, would then illuminate more broadly the shape of all of God's saving purposes."¹³ These practices might be part of what Yoder calls the "grain of the universe." They help to describe the final ends or saving purposes that God intends for human life.

We find quite similar directions in the work of Alexander Schme-

---

9. Karl Barth, *The Christian Life: Church Dogmatics IV.4, Lecture Fragments* (Grand Rapids: Eerdmans, 1981), p. 85.

10. John Howard Yoder, *Body Politics: Five Practices of the Christian Community Before the Watching World* (Nashville: Discipleship Resources, 1994).

11. Yoder, *Body Politics*, pp. 74-77, 79.

12. Yoder, *Body Politics*, pp. 72, 73.

13. Yoder, *Body Politics*, p. 80. Cf. also his final sentence on p. 80: "Why should it not be the case that God's purpose for the world would pursue an organic logic through history and across the agenda of the pilgrim people's social existence with such a reliable rhythm as we have here observed?"

mann, a leading Russian Orthodox theologian. Schmemann prefaces his book *The Eucharist: Sacrament of the Kingdom* with comments about the ethical state of the world. He writes, "It can be said without exaggeration that we live in a frightening and spiritually dangerous age. It is frightening not just because of its hatred, division, and bloodshed. It is frightening above all because it is characterized by a mounting rebellion against God and his kingdom."[14] Schmemann believes that ethical answers to this terrible state of the world are found within the structure and actions of the Eucharistic liturgy. While he admits that the entire Orthodox liturgy has in practice been misunderstood as a pious personal encounter with God, he argues that this understanding is in contrast to the very words and actions of that liturgy. For Schmemann, the way to be relevant to the world is to more deeply embody the final ends of human life that are embedded in and revealed through our worship life. The liturgy is about the formation of the church into the Body of Christ, as Schmemann puts it, "for the life of the world," not as a way to escape it.

In *The Eucharist*, he outlines no less than *twelve* crucial moments in the liturgy in which the patterns of human activity are united to those of God, and calls all of these twelve moments "sacraments." Included in these twelve are the sacrament of the assembly, the sacrament of the offering, the sacrament of the Word, and the sacrament of communion.[15] He understands that in *each* of these acts or practices the activity of the church is "gathered up" into the kingdom of Christ; the patterns of activity of all the people and elements involved are "sanctified" or reshaped to their proper ends. In this way we are given a foretaste of the coming

14. Alexander Schmemann, *The Eucharist: Sacrament of the Kingdom* (Crestwood, N.Y.: St. Vladimir's Seminary Press, 1988), pp. 9-10.

15. A good example of why Schmemann perceives these all as sacraments is seen in his description of the bringing up of the gifts to the altar: "The meaning of this consists in the fact that the offering of *each*, included in the offering of *all*, is now being realized as the Church's offering of her very self, and this means Christ, for the Church is his body, and he is the head of the Church. . . . Our sacrifice is the sacrifice of the Church, which is the sacrifice of Christ. Thus, in this triumphant and royal entrance, in this movement of the gifts, is revealed the truly universal significance of the offering, the unification of heaven and earth, the raising up of our life to the kingdom of God" (*The Eucharist*, pp. 122-23).

kingdom, not only in the elements of bread and wine but in all the central actions, relationships, and patterns of activity of the liturgy.

A consideration of the offering in the worship service illustrates how Schmemann understands it as a pattern of ethical activity. In my own experience, I have heard people jokingly refer to their offering as "the price of admission." That description of what is happening defines the logic of this liturgical act in terms of our capitalist economy; we are fitting our liturgical actions into the patterns of our culture. For Schmemann, this is precisely the reverse of what should be happening. He describes the offering as a central representative act of the total offering of ourselves to Christ and to each other. The offering thus becomes *the* economic paradigm, which, I might add, is in marked contrast to the foundational assumption of most of our economic thinking — namely, that individuals are insatiable units of consumption that will always seek after their own self-interest. Instead, this liturgical action may help form our thoughts, hearts, and actions in such a way that we might be enabled to protest against the economic patterns outside of the liturgy in the so-called real world.

While these three theologians approach Christian life and worship from quite different backgrounds, their thinking shares at least two common features. First, they all see certain actions within the worship liturgy as summary actions for the Christian life as a whole. The liturgy summarizes the kingdom of God. Second, these actions are not empty symbolic actions that refer to some real activity elsewhere; rather, they are actions in which God is present in such a way that our lives, hearts, and minds have the possibility of being shaped into the patterns of the kingdom of Christ.

So, if ethics is understood as speaking about a pattern of human life that fulfills the designs for humanity which God intended, then there is no better place to start this discussion than with the liturgy. For in the liturgy, kingdom patterns are described and embodied. It is in this way that liturgy is ethics, for participation in the liturgy helps us see and guides us into the true ends of human life.

Everyday Life in a Liturgical Context

Occasionally, we encounter specific rules and ethical principles in worship. But more importantly, the liturgy sets before us paradigms of exemplary conduct and involves us in a symbolic world that shapes us deeply. These paradigms and this symbolic world can provide a kind of lens through which we view our lives and the world as a whole.[16] As we approach ethical reflection in such a thick context, the way we pose our ethical questions will change significantly. Instead of asking the typical ethical question — "What is the good thing for a human individual to do, given such-and-such an issue?" — in a liturgical context, this ethical question becomes, "What must our actions be like, both individually and corporately, so as not to make a mockery of our worship of God?" We must ask about the *fittingness* of all our actions in light of our worship before God.

One can step through the many moments of the liturgy to begin to see practical ways in which these regular practices shape our lives as a whole — as has already been seen throughout the previous chapters of this book.[17] For example, the regular practice of confession of sin and assurance of pardon is a powerful practice that shapes us in many ways. Whether done with a single priest or spiritual director as preparation for public worship, as part of written communal confession, or as a public confession to one another within a service, confession creates an awareness of our responsibility to God and one another for our actions. The activity of confession and absolution can and should become a para-

16. In *The Moral Vision of the New Testament* (New York: HarperCollins, 1996), Richard Hays describes the four different "modes of appropriation" of the Scriptures (pp. 208-9). The same four modes can be helpfully applied to the liturgy as a whole.

17. See also the growing theological literature that centers on the idea of formative Christian practices. The following collections are good ways to enter: *Practicing Theology: Beliefs and Practices in Christian Life*, ed. Miroslav Volf and Dorothy C. Bass (Grand Rapids: Eerdmans, 2002); *Knowing the Triune God: The Work of the Spirit in the Practices of the Church*, ed. James J. Buckley and David S. Yeago (Grand Rapids: Eerdmans, 2001); and *Practicing Our Faith: A Way of Life for a Searching People*, ed. Dorothy C. Bass (San Francisco: Jossey-Bass Publishers, 1997).

digm for the way we deal with the conflict, disappointment, and hurt that inevitably enters into all our relationships as fallen creatures.

In and through the liturgy, we are initiated into the practices of confession, forgiveness, and reconciliation. While confession and absolution function as a general interpersonal paradigm, our "liturgical education" about which specific sins to confess also helps us grow in our discernment of the ways of God and the ways we fall short individually and communally. The medieval confessional manuals can be seen as precursors to modern books on Christian ethics.

The act of reading and attending to Scripture, and in some instances the words, responses, and actions that frame these readings (such as "The Word of the Lord" and "Thanks be to God"), not only informs us through the content of the readings but also is a way that the authority of God's Word over our lives is established. In an age where individual autonomy reigns supreme, these acts of worship, submission, and attention shape us in ways that are both explicit and implicit.

The common practice of passing the peace of Christ in quite a practical way trains the community to *be* a community. I have on many occasions heard people say that it was in that moment that they realized they must reconcile with their brother or sister. And in some cases, it was in that moment in the service that a word or nonverbal message was communicated between them that began a reconciliation process. In addition, the discomfort we feel with greeting one another both reveals and challenges the social, racial, and class divisions that exist in our churches.

> **In corporate worship, Christians engage in activities which articulate and shape how they are to be disposed toward the world.**
>
> Don Saliers

Entering into the prayers of the people opens us to the needs of others and habituates us into the activity of being a mediator or an intercessor for others. It can develop our empathy for those in pain. Praying for persons and peoples labeled as our enemies changes us by calling into question the way we easily demonize people, groups, and countries.

The hymns, psalms, and choruses we sing together expose us to and powerfully move us into the full range of Christian experience and emotion — from praise to lamentation. The psalms in particular have been historically understood to be not simply the songs of an individual, but ways that the church as a body expresses the mind and passions of Christ. As we enter into them, our minds and passions are shaped by the patterns of Christ.

And finally, the Eucharist has often been seen as the pinnacle of Christian corporate worship. Its many meanings defy any simple formula, and for some the moments mentioned above are also seen as part of the larger Eucharistic celebration. But at least part of its function is that in the complex of actions and words that make up the celebration, the "final ends" of humanity — the final communion between God, human community, and creaturely elements — are witnessed to, and in them we also gain a foretaste of the feast to come. These "ends," seen most fully in the life and activity of Jesus Christ, are communicated to us as we partake of and embody the Body of Christ.

Within this meaning-complex of the Eucharist, we also see that the path toward these final ends involves suffering, that the way of discipleship involves taking up our own crosses and following the way of Christ. The practice of the Eucharist may indeed push up against many of our cultural understandings and even some of our theological understandings.

These examples show how a Christian character, way of thinking, and way of life can be formed in us through the various moments of our worship practice. But we can also be guided in our thinking about more specific ethical questions as we place those issues against the ethical horizon formed in us by the Christian worship service.

The offering does not give us any definite rules, but rather gives us a normative horizon for our economic practices and policies. The offering within the worship service is a paradigmatic action. The liturgical action involves physically putting a portion of our money into the offering plate and having those offerings brought up with the bread and wine to the altar, which are then distributed as part of God's life for the world. Thinking about our money against such a backdrop will change us, if we have "ears to hear" and "eyes to see." We see money not merely as a means to our pleasure, but begin to see the "true" ends and purposes of money. It is, or can be, a tool that enables us to participate in the ongoing good work of the kingdom.

The recent Catholic social encyclicals, *Laborens Exercens* (1981) and *Centesimus Annus* (1991), reflect an understanding of money and private property that can be said to be "fitting" with such a Eucharistic practice. Ownership of the means of production, for example, is considered "just and legitimate" only insofar as it is placed in service of the right ends — namely, "useful work." "It becomes illegitimate, however, when it is not utilized or when it serves to impede the work of others, in an effort to gain a profit which is not the result of the overall expansion of work and the wealth of society. . . . Ownership of this kind has no justification, and represents an abuse in the sight of God and man."[18] In the light of our practice of the Eucharist, we see that goods are meant not only for ourselves but also for the common good of our sisters and brothers.

Our practices of dating and marriage are another example. Marriage, as it is framed within the pseudo-liturgy of Hollywood film romance, is about finding that special person who will be our all-in-all, that person who fulfills all our needs and desires. Like Jerry McGuire, we must find that person to whom we can say, "You complete me." Looking at marriage against the horizon of baptism, however, we are pulled in a different direction. Rather than looking for someone to complete our bodies, in baptism we immediately recognize that we are called to help complete the body of the church, that the church is our primary family. In fact, baptism tells us that we do not necessarily have to get married at all to live a full Christian life. Christian baptism creates singleness as a second equal option. Whether our baptismal communities are currently sufficient to sustain a meaningful practice of Christian singleness is another question. But the ethics of baptism at least alerts us that we are called to do so as a church. To fill out our understanding of marriage itself, however, we would need to examine the

18. *Centesimus Annus*, par. 43.

marriage liturgy, which in some Christian traditions is tied to the sacrament of the Eucharist.[19]

What about our current American practice of war? Can Christians fight for America, and if so, in what circumstances? How do we decide? Looking at the practice of war in light of our practice of the Eucharist raises interesting questions. At the banquet feast of the Lamb, we gain the eyes to see that Christ has paid the price for our violence and calls us into his Kingdom of Peace in which all peoples are bound together. It becomes more difficult to justify our violence when it is viewed from this perspective than, say, from the perspective of the principle of the greatest good for the greatest number. Stanley Hauerwas asks us "to consider whether Christians can get up from the meal in which Jesus has been the host and begin to kill one another in the name of national loyalties."[20] If indeed in the Eucharist we are in touch with the "really real," perhaps the phrase "political realism" takes on new meaning. At least the burden of proof has shifted.

From these examples, we see that the liturgy cannot be used as an "ethics machine" into which we put an ethical question and out of which pops the Christian answer. Instead, the liturgy provides a guiding horizon that both reframes our questions and guides our thinking in certain directions. It is not our only norm; however, it does provide a normative context in which to do our ethical thinking and acting.

The Charge and the Blessing

Returning to the ending of the liturgy, we can now ask how we might act in ways that will both sum up what has been going on in the liturgy as a

19. See, for example, Paul Evdokimov, *The Sacrament of Love: The Nuptial Mystery in the Light of the Orthodox Tradition* (Crestwood, N.Y.: St. Vladimir's Seminary Press, 2001), and Vigen Guroian, *Incarnate Love: Essays in Orthodox Ethics* (Notre Dame: University of Notre Dame Press, 1987); both authors unpack the meaning of marriage in light of the Eastern Orthodox liturgy of marriage. This includes the celebration of the Eucharist as well as a "crowning" ceremony that indicates marriage as a kind of martyrdom.

20. Hauerwas, "The Liturgical Shape of the Christian Life," p. 16.

whole and alert us to the possibilities of taking the results of our encounter with God into the rest of our lives. In light of the previous discussions, we should ask these questions about the endings of our services: Does this way of ending the service reflect a "centrifugal" understanding of the relationship of liturgy to the rest of life? In other words, can our endings alert us to the fact that in the liturgy we have come in contact with the "really real"? Can the rest of our lives become more self-consciously "real" the more they are lived in ways that correspond to the patterns of Christ which shine forth in our liturgical patterns? Can our lives be liturgies after the Liturgy?

At the beginning of this chapter, I began by relating a few of my worship experiences that I found less than ideal. The endings of those services, while perhaps fitting for what those services conveyed to me as a whole, were not, it seems to me, reflective of what our worship of God can be. But the endings of the services of two other churches I have been part of, while very different in style, reflect these larger liturgical patterns and dynamics quite well.

In the more traditional one, Father Steven, an Episcopal priest, would raise his hands in the sign of blessing. He would then pronounce a traditional benediction such as "The peace of God, which passes all understanding, keep your hearts and minds in the knowledge and love of God, and of his Son Jesus Christ our Lord; and the blessing of God Almighty, the Father, the Son, and the Holy Spirit, be among you, and remain with you always." This would be followed by a call to action, often called a "charge," given by Deacon Betty, a woman well-known for her service of mercy and compassion throughout the community. She would say something like "Let us go forth into the world, rejoicing in the power of the Spirit." The congregation would respond by saying, "Thanks be to God — Alleluia!" and would join in a final hymn as the cross would be carried out, leading the presiding ministers and the rest of the congregation out the center aisle of the sanctuary and into the world. The sense that God had been at work in us and would empower us to live out that charge was powerfully present in those services as a whole and was reflected in that typical ending.

A closer look at the different parts of that particular ending will reveal its theological foundations. It began with a blessing. While the endings of traditional services have varied quite a bit and included many different elements, the blessing is the one common element that is almost always included.[21]

And yet the blessing is an element of the service that makes many pastors feel uncomfortable. Peter Brunner, however, takes it as a "lack of faith" when pastors fail to deliver the blessing in direct speech — "The Lord bless you" — and out of a lack of faith, or failure of nerve, change it to "May the Lord bless us."[22] One reason for this discomfort is that we are unclear what we are asking for. This confusion is often coupled with the lingering suspicion that "blessings" are dead symbolic actions that are not directly related to the action of God, or perhaps that one is demanding from God some kind of "miracle" right then and there.

So what is a blessing? Schmemann says, "God blesses everything He creates, and in biblical language, this means that He makes all creation the sign and means of His presence and wisdom, love and revelation: 'O taste and see that the Lord is good.'"[23] This understanding centers on the acknowledgment of the blessedness of God, the source of all life and blessing. The blessing of food or people thus means that we ask God to make the food or people in some way reflect that blessedness or goodness of God to the extent that is fitting for each. The one blessing is in this way acting as a minister of the Word of God — calling on God to inscribe the patterns or ways of God onto creatures. "Bless this food" — make it serve its proper function to the glory of God. "The Lord bless you" — make these people the salt of the earth, a city on a hill proclaiming the light and glory of the heavenly kingdom through their transfigured lives.

21. Jean-Jacques von Allmen, *Worship: Its Theology and Practice* (Oxford: Oxford University Press, 1968), p. 138.

22. Peter Brunner, *Worship in the Name of Jesus*, trans. M. H. Bertram (Saint Louis: Concordia Publishing House, 1968), p. 135. Von Allmen is even more stringent in his criticism: "Those ministers who transform the proclamation into a wish expressed in the first-person plural are not showing humility, but sabotaging the liturgy, depriving the faithful of part of the grace which God wills to give them" (*Worship*, p. 142).

23. Schmemann, *For the Life of the World: Sacraments and Orthodoxy* (Crestwood, N.Y.: St. Vladimir's Seminary Press, 2000), p. 14.

This understanding is reflected in many traditional prayers of blessing. Blessings have traditionally been a way of marking an object or person "for participation in the divine life." For inanimate objects, blessings have been understood to call for "an influx of the divine life with the aim of cooperating more perfectly with the life of the spirit." For people, blessings have called forth the same "influx of divine life" with the aim of their participating in that life.[24]

Thus, the act of blessing is a kind of epiclesis, a *Maranatha*, a calling for the Holy Spirit to come and transform us. Being blessed by God means that we become holy, reflective of God and the purposes of God. Asking for God's blessing does not mean that we are asking God to somehow help us to achieve our own wants and desires that may be reflective of a sinful culture. Instead, God's blessing means that our wants and desires are "blessed" and made to conform to the will of God. In this conformity to the ways and patterns

> This transformation, remembered, performed, longed for in the liturgy, is the wellspring of desires for the liberation of all that suffers.
>
> Rebecca Chopp

of God, we experience true human blessing and happiness. God does not bless us by fulfilling our own visions of what will make us happy, except to the extent that we are seeking first God's kingdom on earth as it is in heaven.

Thus the blessing, taken by itself and understood in this way, is certainly reflective of the action of God throughout the service that "blesses" us by incorporating us into the patterns of God's purposes and character. In its most traditional uses, it has been meant to remember the final blessing of Christ that he bestowed on his disciples at the time of his ascension. In the event of the benediction in our worship services, the Word of God meets us through the words of the pastor. One liturgi-

---

24. Cyprian Vagaggini, O.S.B., *Theological Dimensions of the Liturgy: A General Treatise on the Theology of the Liturgy*, trans. Leonard Doyle and W. A. Jurgens (Collegeville, Minn.: Liturgical Press, 1976), p. 87.

cal theologian comments, "The blessing is a word charged with power," because in these words God "transmits to persons, living beings or things, salvation, welfare and the joy of living."[25]

Given this understanding, the blessing surely seems to sum up an important purpose of the service as a whole. However, taken by itself, it is unclear to me that the blessing conveys the analogical relationship between the Liturgy and the liturgy of the rest of our lives. The blessing coupled with the "charge" and some action such as a recessional during a final hymn conveys that the liturgy is in one sense over, and yet in another sense is "open-ended." The patterns of the liturgy, the patterns that stem from God's own triune activity, should be embodied not only in the liturgy but also in the whole of our lives and in all the world until all the world reflects the Lordship of Christ. The liturgical cluster of charge and blessing, and perhaps a recessional hymn, effectively embodies God's call to us to faithful obedience and God's sure promise of grace to sustain us daily in that call.

But the basic patterns of "charge" and "blessing" need not be done in traditional ways to be effective. In another congregation I have been part of, the endings of the services exemplify the deeper meanings of our corporate worship quite well in a less traditional form. This congregation is a bilingual congregation whose bilingual services are quite loose and informal in many ways. The ending of the service, however, is often the most formalized part. Immediately before the blessing, the people often stand and sing a chorus in Spanish, then in English that has these words: "I want to be, O my loving Lord, like a vessel in the hands of the potter. So take my life, Lord. Make it anew. I want to be a brand-new vessel." At that point the pastor lifts up his arms and pronounces a blessing over the people. A favorite of his is an adaptation of 2 Corinthians 4:6, which itself alludes to Genesis 1:3, Psalm 112:4, and Isaiah 9:2: "May the God who said, 'Let light shine out of darkness,' shine in your hearts to give the light of the knowledge of the glory of God in the face of Jesus Christ."

The words of the song as well as the words of the blessing embody some of the "final ends" of our worship service as well as that of all hu-

25. Vagaggini, *Theological Dimensions of the Liturgy*, p. 142.

man life. The blessing that is pronounced calls on God to shine in the deepest parts of us with the overall patterns of God reflected in Christ, so that we too might be lights in this world. The "gift" of God that is to be given is that we, like Christ, will become "living sacrifices." After that blessing, the pastor then points us toward the rest of life by saying, "And your response is . . . " — there he often gives a pregnant pause, and then concludes — ". . . to greet each other." It is an atypical and informal way to end, but given that a primary ministry of that church is racial reconciliation and fellowship of the people who make up the congregation, it is an appropriate ending. Occasionally he changes the "charge" and says, "And your response is . . . to stay and enjoy the potluck." The fabulous potlucks of that congregation, which feature the ethnic cuisines of the people, are a community-building activity of the church. Those potlucks are often spoken of as being an extension of the Eucharist, similar to the *agape* feasts of the early church. Again, such an ending points to the way that our liturgical life flows into and transforms all of life.

In both traditional and less traditional ways, the endings of those services sum up God's work in the liturgy and point to the way that God's transforming work in us is to be lived out in the rest of our lives, to the glory of the triune God. Such good liturgical work, repeated week by week, is one of the primary means by which God begins and continues that work in us, so that we might live "for the praise of God's glory" until all the world achieves its final ends and is gathered up in Christ (Eph. 1:10-12).

Lord, Whose Love in Humble Service

Lord, whose love in humble service
bore the weight of human need,
who upon the cross, forsaken,
worked your mercy's perfect deed,
we, your servants, bring the worship
not of voice alone, but heart,
consecrating to your purpose
every gift that you impart.

Still your children wander homeless;
still the hungry cry for bread;
still the captives long for freedom;
still in grief we mourn our dead.
As you, Lord, in deep compassion
healed the sick and freed the soul,
use the love your Spirit kindles
still to make your people whole.

As we worship, grant us vision
till your love's revealing light
in its height and depth and greatness
dawns upon our quickened sight,
making known the needs and burdens
your compassion bids us bear,
stirring us to tireless striving,
your abundant life to share.

Called from worship into service,
forward in your name we go,
to the child, the youth, the aged,
love in living deeds to show.
Hope and health, goodwill and comfort,
counsel, aid, and peace we give,
that your children, Lord, in freedom
may your mercy know, and live.

Albert F. Bayly (1901-1984), 1961

Canto de Esperanza/Song of Hope

Dios de la esperanza, danos gozo y paz!
Al mundo en crisis, habla tu verdad.
Dios de la justicia, mándanos tu luz.
Luz y esperanza en la oscuridad.

May the God of hope go with us every day,
filling all our lives with love and joy and peace.
May the God of justice speed us on our way,
bringing light and hope to every land and race.

Estribillo:
Oremos por la paz,
cantemos de tu amor,
luchemos por la paz,
fieles a ti, Señor.

Refrain:
Praying, let us work for peace,
singing, share our joy with all,
working for a world that's new,
faithful when we hear Christ's call.

Dios será nuestro pastor en el camino
no nos abandonará cuando nos perdimos.
La vida es una carga pesada,
Pero Dios siempre nos ayudará.

God will be our Shepherd as we go our way
and will not forsake us when we go astray.
Even though the load of life is hard to bear,
we must not forget that God is always there.

Stanza 1: Spanish traditional, trans. Alvin Schutmaat (1921-1988);
stanza 2: Tom Mitchell (b. 1947), trans. Frank W. Roman (b. 20th c.).